CAN YOU REALLY TALK TO GOD?

LOUIS H. EVANS, SR.

CAN YOU REALLY TALK TO GOD?

WORD BOOKS
PUBLISHER
WACO, TEXAS

CAN YOU REALLY TALK TO GOD?

CONTENTS

1.

WHEN WE PRAY—
A FARCE OR A FORCE?

Is It a Pose or a Power?

IN THIS BOOK we shall be matching our minds and souls with some breathtaking promises: "If we ask anything according to his will he hears us" (1 John 5:14); "Everyone who asks receives" (Matt. 7:8, RSV). These are stupendous, powerful words—blasphemous if they are wrong, and arrogant; but mighty and fraught with privilege if they are right. Thomas Carlyle once said, "Prayer lives and remains the native and deepest impulse of man."

Have you and I, finite beings, the right to tap the infinite resources of an infinite God? Will his eternal ear hear our humble cry? Would the God of all creation, who tossed the moon and stars into their orbits and presides over the light-years of space, be affected by our desires—stoop to our human needs? If this is true, we must move up on it! To miss the use of this Power would be insane, foolish, and frustrating.

Prayer, then, is a problem of our day and any day in history. This brings to mind some words I once read: "The problem of prayer: It has been a long time coming, but here it is all at once in its very starkness. Like a flash in the night it throws into vivid relief the nature of the struggle, full of power or paradox and the danger with which religious thought is daily involved. The problem of prayer: That is the critical issue. There the most desperate conflict between the friends and foes of religion will be fought. The attitude which theology takes toward this issue [of prayer] will determine in large degree the future of Christianity in the world." Yes, our future in this world and the next!

Is this power to talk with God—to use the power of God—merely a "wish-fancy"? Does he hear? Does he care? Could prayer move mountains, send rain upon parched fields, turn back armies, change destinies of men, save souls, cleanse lives, and bless homes? When we pray is the act a farce or a force—a pose or a power?

The lifting power of prayer depends, to a great extent, *on our faith in it*. To lift, a lever must rest upon a fulcrum. The lift of prayer must rest upon the fulcrum of faith—a series of convictions and sureties concerning prayer. Our confidence in prayer will be made up partially of answers to *weighty* questions.

First: CAN GOD ANSWER PRAYER? It seems

presumptuous to even think that the Creator of the universe must remain dumb, deaf, and blind in the midst of it. Has he made his laws of nature his own jailors?

If man with his comparatively puny mind can take God-given resources and create copper wire, steel, and glass and then make them into a Telestar or television set through which we can speak to the world and to each other by tossing our voices across mountain ranges and seas, could God not converse with his children when they cry—or answer when they call?

> If radio's slim fingers can pluck a melody
> From night and toss it over a continent or sea:
> If the petalled white notes of a violin
> Are blown across a mountain or a city's din;
> If songs like crimson waves are culled
> From thin blue air; why should mortals wonder
> If God answers prayer?
>
> Ethel Romig Fuller

Second: WILL HE HEAR AND ANSWER? It depends upon who you think God is. Are you a deist or a theist? A deist believes that there is a God, that He created the universe with its natural laws but has little to do with it now. He has left it to its own devices. God is the inventor, but not the engineer. Do not expect him to tamper with it. Prayer alters nothing.

The theist on the other hand believes that God not only "made the watch," but is also "the jeweler." He is a God of repair, rewinding his creation with his divine energy, resetting errant human hands.

Christ said, "When you pray, say: '*Our Father*'" (Luke 11:2, NKJV). As a father, he does not wrap himself up in the robe of indifference like an impersonal, aloof monarch allowing his children to cry to him unaided and unheard. As a heavenly father he is "touched with the feeling of our infirmities" (Heb. 4:15, KJV). He is not impersonally deaf to our cries.

Third: WILL GOD BREAK HIS LAWS TO ANSWER OUR PRAYERS? Dare we ask for "miracles" that demand that God defy his laws?

In a sense, *some* "miracles" are the *seeming* violation of natural law. But, in fact, they are the result of other laws interacting in an orderly fashion. If you, as a father, were walking along with your son beside new buildings which were under construction, and looking up, you saw a brick falling which, according to the law of height and gravity, might strike him and bring injury, naturally you would put out your hand and, if possible, deflect its natural fall. Have you broken the law of gravity? No, you are merely bringing into action another force—the power of your hand—to counteract the law of gravity in an orderly fashion. God's hand is not straitened that it cannot save!

When you summon the doctor to arrest that disease which, according to natural law, may

bring about your death, are you asking him to
break the laws of physiology? No. Through his
study he has discovered other laws which are
able to counteract those laws of decay and in an
orderly way arrest the disease. He is bringing
into play certain laws of health and healing of
which we are ignorant. Christ, in some of his
healings, may have employed laws known but to
him and foreign to us, since there dwelt in him
"the fullness of the Godhead bodily" (Col. 2:9,
NKJV). The doctor's predicament has often become Christ's opportunity. A plane in the air a
century ago, being "heavier than air" would
have been a law-breaking miracle. But now we
have learned of new laws of aviation stronger
than the laws of gravity, making the "impossible" flight of yesterday the orderly habit of today. Thomas Huxley once said that, "law was
established by what we observed would happen
in the *usual number of cases.*" But is God not
able to do the *unusual* when the situation demands it?

If a ship is on its decided course at a decided
speed and the cry is heard, "Man overboard!" is
the captain breaking the laws of navigation
when suddenly he flashes to the engine room,
"Full speed astern," and stops the orderly
course of the ocean liner for the saving of a
passenger? Is the captain on the bridge in control, or is he the slave of the ordinary schedule of
his ship?

When I was visiting one of the colonies of Britain, in a certain city the traffic laws were suspended because the King's son, the Prince of Wales, was for the first time visiting that part of his domain. Ordinary traffic laws were suspended. Soon afterward the laws were restored. Was that edict of the king permissible? "Once at the end of the ages [Christ] has appeared to put away sin by the sacrifice of Himself [in His death]" (Heb. 9:26, NKJV). The Father's love had invaded this world with the Prince of Heaven in the Incarnation. In the Virgin Birth, the ordinary laws of conception and birth were arrested to make possible the coming of the Son of God. Never before had he been "made flesh," therefore, who could establish the law as to how this would be accomplished? God felt that our justification from sin by the Savior of the world would make this necessary and right.

Again, Christ would make his resurrection from the dead, beyond a doubt, the Father's imprimatur and stamp of approval on his saviorship, thus assuring us that his power to overcome physical death would verify his power to overcome spiritual death—the separation of our souls from God.

The atheists and deistic naturalists, who insist on living in a walled-in universe in which God is a captive of the laws of usual occurrence, his own "laws being his jailors," will often boggle at the supernatural and make their God nature's slave.

If the Creator has made it possible for the death-dealing malignancy of cancer to be arrested by the lawful use of radium, and he lets the power of intercessory prayer defeat the law of sin and death and "save the sick," then let us keep praying.

Fourth: SHALL I USE WHAT I DO NOT UNDERSTAND? I cannot understand this force of prayer. Dare I trust it then?

Did the South Sea natives dare to use the wind to fill their sails and waft them to their destinations before they had read a book on the physics of wind? How dare you take the phone and expect to hear another voice if you do not understand telephony? Is not the right yours because you ask and receive an answer? How dare you switch on the light and flood your room with it unless you understand electricity? The flood of light justifies your right. Because the babe does not understand the mysteries of nourishment and the gustatory exercise, should it not imbibe of breast or bottle? Does a lack of understanding of the life combustion that makes that planted seed become his harvest cause the farmer to refuse to sow his fields? If we cannot fully understand the mystery of conception and birth, do we deny the possibility of new birth when prayer pleads for and expects it at the hand of God? We may experience prayer without understanding it!

Asking is God's law of receiving. Ask and you shall receive; knock and it shall be opened. You receive not because you ask not.

There are reasons for praying other than those intimated in the preceding pages.

First: PRAYER WAS REQUIRED OF CHRIST. "In the days of his flesh, Jesus offered up prayers and supplications, with loud cries and tears to him who was able to save him from death, and he was heard for his godly fear" (Heb. 5:7, RSV). In his daily life and times of crisis he talked with God.

I like what the famous Charles Spurgeon said, "Whether we like it or not, asking is the rule of the Kingdom. 'Ask and you will receive' is never to be altered in anyone's case. God has not relaxed that rule for Jesus Christ the Elder Brother. If the royal Son of God cannot be exempted from this rule of asking that he might have, you and I cannot expect this rule to be relaxed in our favor. Why should it be? If you have everything by asking and nothing by not asking, you can see how vital prayer is." Christ is still at the right hand of God making intercession for us. Prayer was and is still his lifestyle.

Second: PRAYER IS NECESSARY BECAUSE OF WHAT WE ARE. If we are conscious that we are made "in the image of God," then two dynamic aims pervade our lives: I would be perfect even as my Father in heaven is perfect (Matt. 5:48) and "to me to live is Christ" (Phil. 1:21, KJV). If we say we can get along without prayer, then we are not getting along at all. If we are prayerless, then our egotistic humanity ought to rub its eyes and become conscious of its moral and spiritual inadequacy in the sight of God.

You can get along without prayer—without speaking to God or letting God speak to you—but without his help, don't undertake anything that takes unusual courage of soul. Don't try to do much for the church or the world; don't ever try to be different from the mob out there. Just go about your business, making a living, though not a life. Try to live on your income; pick out the jobs that are just your size and let the rest go. Travel a mediocre road. Imagine you are living when you are just existing, and you'll get along without God and prayer. But try to be what he asks you to be, different and mighty; try to beat down selfishness for greatness of heart; try to master that temper and most of all yourself; try to live a life that will be shockingly different because of its purity and courage; try to be a model for your children—then you will cry out to God, all right, and find yourself singing, "Leaning on the Everlasting Arms."

Third: WE NEED PRAYER BECAUSE OF WHAT THE CHURCH IS. The main aim of the church

collectively is the same as your aim
personally—"Seek ye first the kingdom of God,
and his righteousness" (Matt. 6:33, KJV). However we may be making a living—this is what
we are living for. Without the help and guidance
of prayer, we are like a train without tracks, a
car without a driver, a ship without a compass,
a scholar without a teacher.

The early church had little to which we give
the palm today. Its budget seemed trivial al-
though the giving of its individual members
shocked the Roman world by its selflessness. Its
membership was not outstanding across the
board for its wise men, kings, emperors, rich
folks, and the mighty. These would come later,
many of them. He chose "the foolish to con-
found the wise." For the most part they were
fishermen, tax collectors, housekeepers of
Bethany; mixed here and there with a Paul—a
triple-A scholar—or a wealthy woman named
Salome, or a Lydia, or a Centurion. But its
vitality lay not mainly in its people, but in their
prayer power. As to buildings, often they had
none. They met in homes, on hillsides, in caves,
in catacombs, cellars—in a "city beneath the
city" of Rome. But because they praised and
prayed, they soon emptied the thrones of Rome
and placed a Christian Caesar there.

The Church is the Body of Christ. What breath
is to the body, prayer is to the soul. When we

stop breathing, physically we die. When we stop praying, spiritually we die. A prayerless Christian is a breathless Christian, and breathless people never do their best work. The church at its best must use its prayer power.

The prayerless Christian is like the boatman who had been frantically rowing his sailboat for hours. At last, with blistered hands, he breathlessly grasped the dock. A friend on the wharf helping him make fast his boat glanced at the furled, unused sails lying on the boat bottom. In dismay he exclaimed, "Man, why didn't you put up the sails and use the wind?" Sheepishly he exclaimed, "I forgot."

How often does a church, depending upon a pompous program, teeming with talent, proud of its members, balancing its budget, enlisting its converted crew, earnestly teaching and trying, preaching and persuading, find itself exhausted simply because it forgot to unfurl the sails of prayer and use fully the mighty winds of God. "More things are wrought by prayer than this world dreams of"—or more than some Christians are aware of.

Fourth: PRAYER SHOULD BE OUR NATURAL CARRIAGE—as natural as breathing. Some people use God only as a "divine aspirin tablet." They only run to him in times of pain and heartache and danger. Such was the case in the following shipwreck incident:

One of the lifeboats from the already sunken ship was crammed with frightened passengers, fearful of being swamped. One of them said to the first mate in command of the lifeboat, "You are first in command here, and it's your duty to care for the spiritual life and safety of the passengers. Say a prayer, man. Say a prayer!" Bewildered, the mate, unused to praying or any religious exercise, blurted out, "God, you know I've never talked to you before, but I promise you this: get us out of this mess, and I'll never bother you again!"

Tragic escapists like the first mate unfairly call upon a God whom they have never permitted to call upon them.

We shall never be able to be "men for all seasons" or "women for all situations" or "youth for all occasions" until our ability to call upon God and God's ability to call upon us become the alternate beats of the vital heart of our faith.

The vitality of the early church, as we have said, was found not so much in its budget, its size, its membership, its program, or in the structure that housed it; but in its prayer life. When Peter was miraculously delivered from prison and "the doors opened of their own accord," he was swift to guess the cause of his release. He went immediately to his company and found that they had been praying.

When the First Presbyterian Church of Hollywood suddenly found itself to be the largest Presbyterian Church in America, several journalists asked me to explain this phenomenon. One even asked, "How did you do it?" To which I immediately answered, "I had practically nothing to do with that; the Holy Spirit happened to choose this corner to evidence his power." But some would doggedly ask another question, insisting that there must have been some human elements or practical factors in its growth. I insisted that these, too, would be Spirit-inspired and Spirit-used—and that one of these was prayer.

Some seventeen-hundred members signed up to become a part of a great "cordon of prayer"—each pledging to pray daily for some specific person or phase of the program. They were organized into "cells of seven" which met weekly in prayer, because Christ has promised "where two or three are gathered together in my name, there am I in the midst of them" (Matt. 18:20, KJV). Ten of these cells would meet together once a month as a "block of prayer" numbering some seventy people. Once a year the entire cordon would meet. Several secretaries volunteered to register and record the many answers to prayer that were reported. The records became too large to handle and the people were asked simply to be sure that God was answering their requests in surprising ways. The elders' wives were organized in a prayer block of fifty, and within a half hour after some emergency arose they were all praying the same request.

Was it easy to so engage people in prayer? Certainly not. It was one of the most difficult requests Christ made of his disciples.

When preparing for the Gethsemane experience and his own prayer-struggle, Christ asked his favorite disciples to tarry in prayer while he went alone to talk with the Father. But when he came back an hour later, he found them asleep—his most faithful disciples. It seemed they would march for him, talk for him, witness for him, work for him, suffer for him, and even die for him—everything but pray for him.

No amount of organization, ecclesiastical stewardship, or experience—no program—can take the place of prayer. One man said, "In my church, we are so well organized, there is 'so much harness you can hardly find the horse.'" It is no little thing when a member says to a pastor, "I am praying for you." It's a Christian's greatest gift. It usually happens that a puny preacher is backed by a prayerless pew, while a powerful preacher is backed by praying pews.

May God teach us how to use this greatest privilege and power of prayer to weigh our successes, appraise our failures, lengthen our stakes, enlarge the audible spectrum that hears the voice of God, to go on and on to the astonishment of ourselves and our community; and in truth "thus by golden chains we are bound together at the feet of God."

Then prayer shall never be merely a farce, but a force; not simply a pose, but a mighty power!

May I suggest this as our personal prayer: *"Oh, God, thou art love and love seeks an object for that love and thou hast chosen us on whom to bestow that love and the privilege and power of prayer. As to this royal speech with thee, help us to remember always that thou art more anxious to speak to us than we are to speak with thee. Give us then, throughout these pages, this classic confidence that thou wilt hear us. Teach us, then, more and more how to find thee, to hear thee, and to follow thee. Lord, teach us to pray. In the name of Christ—Amen."*

2.

IS THERE ANYBODY THERE?

The Practice of His Presence

ALONG WITH HIS PEACE, his power, his pardon, and his presence, prayer is one of the greatest gifts that God has proffered us. Man, made in God's image, is the only part of creation that can have speech with God. "For what are men better than sheep or goats / That nourish a blind life within the brain, / If, knowing God, they lift not hands of prayer?" Alfred, Lord Tennyson. We are the only creatures who can have conversation with the Creator.

Most people pray or try to pray. Even the atheist has to watch himself. One said, "I don't believe there is a God and I thank God for it." Of course there are some deists who say, "I think there is a God in this universe, but I think he started it like a big machine and then left it alone to its own devices. He never tampers with it now. Natural law has taken over. God has stepped out of the picture, and it is no use trying to get in touch with him." But the theist says that is not true. To him God is not only the inventor of this universe, but he is its engineer. He still has his hand on the throttle. He listens when we talk to him. He is attentive to this world.

We live in a world where, to many, it seems unnatural to pray. Bernhard Iddings Bell said in his book, *Beyond Agnosticism*, "Ours is a steam-heated, well-lighted, cunningly upholstered, warm-bathed era. With almost incredible ingenuity we ward off the bumps, we plane the corners, we escalate the heights; with twilight-sleep birth and narcotisized death we insist upon ease, comfort of body and soul. In such times people are not interested in the sweet bye-and-bye, the sweet now-and-now has their attention. Present comfort eclipses future salvation. They would rather improve the living conditions in the city of destruction than flee from it. The Celestial City is just not on their itinerary. A self-sufficient people have no inclination to seek assistance from without." If prayer is a Christian's vital breath, then some people are still breathless.

John Coburn said, "Prayer for many is like a foreign land. When we go there we go as tourists, and like most tourists we feel uncomfortable and out-of-place. We therefore move on before too long and go somewhere else and do something else. But we must all become native on the significant soil of prayer. We must feel at home on our knees."

Prayer, however, is not real to a lot of people. Sometimes it is a pose instead of a power. One of the difficulties in making prayer real is learning how to *feel the actual presence of God.*

The problem can be seen clearly in the story of the young girl who said, "Sometimes, when I feel a little bit 'Sunday-nightish,' I do kneel down beside my bed, but I soon go woolgathering. I think of my hair-do, my Prince Charming, the junior prom; will I flunk the final? I have sort of given prayer up as an empty business. It didn't seem as if anybody were listening."

Ever feel that way?

A businessman once said to me, "I used to pray, but I have given it up. It didn't seem as if anybody were there." I replied, "Maybe you're right. You can't walk right in on God, you know. *There are conditions for being in God's presence.*"

Often our prayers *are not unto God;* they are *unto people.* You can tell by the way some people pray that it is more to impress people than to impress God. There was a group of some forty businessmen who used to meet on Tuesday noons for prayer. The man who was leading that day said, "Today I don't want one of you men to lead in audible prayer until you actually feel

that you are in the presence of God." He timed
the silence. It was twelve minutes before anyone
spoke! That's a long, long time to wait.

*How can we be sure that we are in the presence
of God*—that Somebody is listening? Christ presents the conditions of this presence in the
Lord's Prayer. Jesus said, "When you pray, say,
'*Our Father.*'" Is not God everybody's Father?
Physically he is a first cause, a provider, a
creator, a giver of life. However, he is not to all a
spiritual "Father." Something has to happen to
you and me before we can say honestly and
spiritually, "Our Father." Of many Jesus said,
"If God were your Father, you would love
me.... You are of your father the devil and your
will is to do your father's desires." (John 8:42,
44; RSV).

In John 1:12 we read, "As many as received
Him, to them He gave the right to *become the
children* of God" (NKJV). We *become* what we
were not before. When that happens we cry
"*Abba, my Father.*" *Abba* means "Papa," very
approachable—"Daddy," reverently said. Then
Jesus Christ becomes our Elder Brother, and
every Christian in the world becomes our
brother or our sister. There is not another organization like that. The church, of course, is a
family. God wants to be everyone's Father, but
not everyone wants to be his child. We have to

want that and move up on it. Jesus said, "No one comes to the Father, but by me" (John 14:6, RSV).

Let's ask what that means, "No one comes to the Father, but by me." Let me illustrate it by sharing with you my son Bill's experience in climbing the Matterhorn. When he was telling me about it he explained how someone said that as you go up to a height of two thousand feet there are maybe six or eight trails you can choose to take. When you get to eight thousand feet there are only about three left. But, if you want to get to the summit of the Matterhorn and stand there with the invigorating wind of victory in your face, then there is only one trail to take. Likewise, Jesus is the only way to the Father.

Prayer is understanding speech with God, but there are various conceptions of God. There are some religions that bring you to a height of two thousand feet and say that God is an impersonal Creator and you are his impersonal creature. Others lead you up to eight thousand feet and say that God is a great sovereign of the world and you are his impersonal subject. But Christ says, "When you pray, say, Our Father." He alone gave us that concept. The true God is your Abba Father, and you are his very precious child. Being able to address God as our Father is the great difference between a Buddhist at his prayerwheel, a Mohammedan on his prayer rug, and a Christian kneeling at the cross.

One day at a military encampment a boy went to the headquarters tent, and to the aide on guard he said, "I want to see the general." The aide-de-camp said, "You can't see him, boy. The general is busy. Run along now." The boy said, "He's my daddy, I guess I can see him, I guess I can!" The aide said, "If he's your daddy, son, walk right in." You can walk right into the presence of God if you can say, "Abba, Father." Can you? We are his and he is ours by the "adoption of faith" in the deepest sense.

According to his will he hears us. "Well, God doesn't answer my prayers," a woman said to her pastor. "Didn't he say if we ask anything according to his will, he hears us?" The pastor said, "Yes, but do you belong to the *we's?*"

As Christians we have some privileges in understanding the desires of God's heart. One is kneeling at the cross in an explained and unusual relationship allowed us by Jesus Christ.

A certain cult says that God is not a personal God—he is a divine Principle—sort of an "It." So this group sees audible prayer as a hindrance—the Divine Being is no "auditory nerve." Prayer to them is meditation, you see. This kind of thinking is like the man who went to his doctor and the doctor said, "Here is what I suggest: I want you to take a walk to that well a mile away to get a drink of water every day before breakfast. There is a well there, but I warn you that there isn't any water in it. But *the walk will do you good!*" The attitude of the cult mentioned here suggests that there is no personal God out there, but the exercise of prayer is beneficial. They call it the "reflex blessing of prayer." You may have that if you want it, but I want to find Somebody at the other end—a Father.

To philosopher Plato, God was an idea, to Hegel God was just a spirit, to Spinoza God was substance, to Schopenhauer God was unconscious will, to Spencer God was the unknowable, and to Kant God was an "intellectual broom with which we sweep up the multiplicity of life's phenomena." Does that warm the cockles of your heart?

"When ye pray, say, Our Father" (Luke 11:2, KJV). There is no need for you women's libbers to worry about the masculine term used here. This is only one of God's characteristics. When a boy is playing with blocks he can only build as large a house as he has blocks with which to build. When he runs out of blocks he stops building. When God explains himself and his attributes, he uses the blocks of experiences which are ours, such as parental relationships. Because he has the attributes of feminine comfort, we

understand him through a mother's love. "As
one whom his mother comforts, so I will comfort you" (Isa. 66:13, RSV). Also we see him
through a father's understanding, "As a father
pities his children, so the Lord pities those who
fear him" (Ps. 103:13, RSV). Christ called the
disciples his "brethren" and we see him
through a brother's constancy and companionship. "Husbands, love your wives, as Christ
loved the church" (Eph. 5:25, RSV). The church
is also the "bride" of Christ. We understand
these metaphors, and they help us have some
knowledge of God and his characteristics as we
address him.

Now let me summarize the conditions for
feeling the presence of God as Christ gives them
in the Lord's Prayer.

First: Do you have this friendly *parental relationship?* Can you honestly say as an act of will,
"God, you are my Father. By an act of will I
become your child"? (See John 1:12; Rom.
8:15.)

Second: We come for *pardon.* "Forgive us our
debts, as we forgive our debtors" (Matt. 6:12,
RSV). God is a holy God and he cannot have fellowship with unholiness. One of the things we
must do is face up to our sins honestly. Rebel-
lion against God is the attitude of sin—the gesture of the clenched fist. The open hands—
praying hands—are the gesture of submission.

Forgive us, Father, as we forgive our debtors and dislodge our enmities.

Third: We have to come to him with the right *purpose.* Why do you want to talk with God? About what do you wish to see him?

"Hallowed be thy name. *Thy kingdom come....*" (Matt. 6:9–10, RSV). What do we mean by that? "*Thy will be done ...*" (Matt. 6:10, RSV). Is that what we crave—"God I want to talk to you about your will, what you want"? Is that the first desire, or is it, "I have something I want"? When you are in a rowboat and you throw out a rope to the dock, what are you trying to do? Are you trying to pull that shoreline over to your boat, or your boat to the shoreline? The answer ought to be evident. So in prayer, which are we trying to do? It depends upon how we pray. Is his will our chief desire, or are we trying to adjust his will to our desires?

When you are driving down the highway with the white line in the middle, does the way you drive your car change the position of the white line, or do you follow the markings by driving on the right side of the line? It will not take long to find out which pays. God, thy will be done.

Often we go to God with a blueprint, "this is what I want," and we do not give him a chance to map out his plans for us and in us. The *surrender of our wills*, then, is also a condition of a talk with God. Kierkegaard said, "A man's prayer does not alter the unalterable. The true explanation, the most desired is: Prayer does not change God—it changes us." We may not be trying to change God's will, but he might be wanting to change ours. We must adjust our will to God's. When we do this, the conversation with him becomes a *revelation of what he wants* for us, rather than a request for what we desire of him.

It has been said that prayer is surrender—an intimate invitation extended to God, privately or collectively, presenting him with the *keys* to our city, the *helm* and *rudder* of the ship of our souls and our lives and saying, "Guide me, God." In prayer, the "I" that is, surrenders to the "I" that ought to be. This is not just self-realization—this is also self-renunciation.

Prayer is a branch surrendering to the vine for strength, a bulb plugging into the socket for light. It is a patient yielding to the doctor for healing. It is a child listening to the teacher for instruction. It is a soldier standing at attention, reporting to the general for orders. Prayer is practicing the luxury of God's guidance. "God, thy will be done." How that changes things.

Fourth: We must *practice the presence of God.* In the phrase, "Our Father who art in all the heavens," the word *heaven* in Hebrew is *hashamayim* (plural). The Hebrews saw the universe as symbolic. There was the "first heaven"—the air they breathed where the trees bloom. Then there was the "second heaven"—the heaven where the rain fell, where the birds made their flight. There was also the higher heaven—stellar space where the moon and stars were which God had ordained. Finally there was the "upper heaven" where God dwelled—but not positionally as to limit God.

God is not limited to a certain place, sitting on a throne, a being with a long white beard. God is incorporeal—without a body. He is omnipresent. What I mean is this, "Our Father who art in all the heavens—You who give us the air we breathe, You who keep the leaves fresh, You who see to the needs of the sparrow, You, God, who drive the moon and the stars in their orbits—hear my prayer. Our Father who in quality is high above all these things, God, who art all and through all, be pleased to hear my prayer."

We must *practice the presence of God* everywhere and always. We need to start in the morning before we are all tuckered out. When you wind your "watch" then, the spring is wound to stand the pounding and banging of the day ahead. If you wind it up at night, the spring will already be weary at dawning and will not stay steady through the day. Likewise, morning prayers give us the power to meet the waking hours and face up to life. They make us attentive and alert to what God and other people are saying.

Muriel Lester wrote: "Start praying in the morning. Immediately, when you wake, set your first thoughts on God. Keep your mind on Him for at least a few moments. Do not think of Him subjectively as to your relation to Him—your sins—your failures—your need; but rather objectively be conscious of Him, His holiness, His love. This is of inevitable importance. It is a habit that is easy to build and sustain after you practice it—it can be comprehended almost instantly as you awake. If unpleasant memories press upon you early in the morning, do not worry about it. Smile and think, 'What a good thing God does not look on me as I look on myself.' He sees something in me thoroughly lovable and He is expecting something worthwhile and fine to work itself out in my life and is waiting for it to show itself. Don't get out of bed until you have set your thought upon God, and consider yourself unready to talk to other people until you have first talked with God. This will give tone to the whole day."

Let us practice the Presence *during the day.* The Scripture passage, "Pray without ceasing" (1 Thess. 5:17, KJV), troubles some people. "What does it mean?" they ask. "Must I keep praying all the time? After all, I have an exam to take—there are dishes to do—I have children to take care of—I must drive to the office—can I park and just stop everything to talk to God?" Certainly we must have periods of silence and inactivity. But to "pray without ceasing" simply may mean that we are to *keep the wire open between God and ourselves* all the time. You can chat with him when you are driving to work—when you are walking to school—while you are taking an exam—when you are working at the sink amid the clatter of the dishes and the humming of the kettle.

One woman said of her kitchen chores, "It's like the music of the seraphim and cherubim." It need not make any difference what position you are in when you pray. One man said, "The finest prayer I ever prayed was when I was stuck head-downward in a well. Did I talk to God!" A cowboy said, "Some of my best prayin' was from my saddle." Another was face-down in a foxhole. One was in a wheelchair. Christ prayed from the cross. Keeping in touch with him constantly during the pressures of the day is to "pray without ceasing."

Practicing the presence of God will give us poise and enable us to adjust ourselves to every situation. But it means learning to "wait upon the Lord" and letting that attitude become part of our natures. Knowing that God is with you is

wonderful therapy for the spirit. It's like a
thermostat which regulates the troubled times
in your life.

The Creator has placed in your body a thermostat that, if working properly, keeps your
temperature at 98.6 degrees, no matter what the
conditions are outside. To get an idea just how
effective this thermostat is, a while back in a
football game between Oklahoma University
and the University of Southern California, it
was 120 degrees in the shade and no shade!
When players were taken out of the game from
exhaustion, the doctor took their temperatures.
They were all 98.6 degrees. Tremendous!

Here's another example of that incredible
body thermostat we have. My first church was
in North Dakota, and they invited me back for
the burning of the mortgage fifty years later.
Many memories flashed across my mind.... A
cyclone had blown down one of the two
churches I was pastoring, and we worshiped in
a consolidated school house. Big, husky, two-
hundred-fifty-pound farmers squeezed into
third-grade desks to worship God. In minus
fifty-two-degree weather, I would look out and
see a sleigh drive up. Then twenty heads would
bob up from the straw and blankets they had
used to keep from freezing. Some of the men
used to go into the basement and stand around
the wood stove to melt the icicles from their

mustaches so that when they sang they would not sound like castanets. But their body temperature was 98.6 degrees. Spiritually speaking, we also come to some viciously hot and cold times in our lives. We are fatigued with the sweat and the heat of the commonplace and nearly frozen by the chilling discouragement of utter disappointment. Have you God's thermostat when there is treason somewhere—when there is no love in the home or when there is failure in business or health? Have you the poise of prayer?

When David found his son, Absalom, organizing an army to march against him and seize his throne he did not go to pieces. In Psalm 3:4–5, David said, "I cried unto the Lord. . . . I laid me down and slept; I awaked; for the Lord sustained me" (KJV). In Psalms 4 we see clearly that when David prayed and put his trust in God he was able to sleep peacefully. God's thermostat again!

Like David, we in today's troubled world need to pray and trust God. In one of my former churches there was a crack salesman who had won two awards for sales, but he had been neglecting the church and had little time for prayer. Then he had a nervous breakdown and was on his back for six months. When he was back at his office, I went to see him. He said, "I'm okay again, Louie." I asked, "What's the secret?" He said, "Stillness. With all the competition in business, I didn't take time to catch my breath spiritually." He went on to explain that what breath is to your body, prayer is to your soul. Stop breathing and you die physically. Stop praying and you die spiritually. Then he said "I had forgotten to breathe." He took down a devotional book, "Now I say to my secretary, 'Don't interrupt me for fifteen minutes.' I read Scripture and the explanation of Scripture, and then I talk to God for five minutes. And now I'm all right. It's stillness, Louie."

A small boy suffered from a bad heart. His mother would see a flare-up coming and would motion him over to her lap. He would leave his toys and climb up in her lap, put one chubby hand over one ear to shut out the noise, and press the other ear close to his mother's heart. When he heard her heartbeat, his own little heart began to slow down and beat strongly, steadily—just like his mother's. There come times when we must get very close to God to keep our hearts beating with courage and strength.

The Holy Spirit says to us:

Come you yourselves apart and rest awhile.
Weary, I know it, of this press and throng.
Wipe from your brow this dust and sweat of toil
And in My quiet strength be strong.
Come you and rest. This journey is too great

And you will fall beside the way and sink.
The bread of life is here for you to eat
And here the wine of love for you to drink.
Then, fresh from converse with your Lord,
Rise, and work till daylight softens into even;
That hour was not lost in which you learned
More of your Master and His rest in heaven.

AUTHOR UNKNOWN

Be sure to *end the day with prayer.* In *Ways of Praying,* Muriel Lester says: "Never get into bed with a burdened or a heavy mind. Take your problem and talk it over with God. That oppression, that definite fear, get rid of that evil thing before you lie down and sleep. Better to spend fifteen minutes to talk it out with God than to toss on a pillow sleeplessly all night. God will take care of it for you before you slumber." Face it—share the burden. It's half as heavy if you let God carry the other end.

One Christian prayed at the close of day: "The anger I felt this morning, God, was like murder. It could have been murder. It did real harm to the person I vented it upon; others are reacting to it still. It was anti-social, a sin. God forgive me. It is not just remission of penalty I am asking for when I say, 'forgive;' it is a longing to be whole again, a passionate desire to save my victim from the consequences of my anger, a willingness to do anything to make amends.

"Father, anger is a force, and I have let it loose

upon the world; it may have wrecked the happiness of several people. Have mercy upon me, sinner, weakling, fool that I am! Let Christ's love undo the harm I have done. Let his love save and redeem my victim. Goodnight, God."

Tonight we may do something to allay the pain, restore the friendship and mend the breakage. But tonight's *prayer* may bring more rest than *pills.*

Let us pray with a mighty *confidence in God and tomorrow.* "For thine is the kingdom and the power and the glory, forever, Amen" (Matt. 6:13, KJV). We must *believe* that.

Arnold J. Toynbee in his *A Study of History—Withdrawal and Return* (Oxford University Press) writes: "Each great leader has first taken time out by himself to be alone. Then when he was full of new vision he came back and led the people, sometimes by the millions. Most of these movements lasted long after the founders were dead. When they were alone, they had some kind of deep experience and here is what is the most important. Many of these men of world-changing power were without much education, background or importance before they went off by themselves. Apparently they became so absorbed in great concepts that they lost their sense of egocentric self-consciousness. God can do anything with anyone who gives Him the first chance at his life and motivation. Without this, one's courage can pale."

During the years when I was acting as summer supply at the National Presbyterian Church in Washington, D.C., the President and Mrs. Eisenhower invited my wife and me over for tea at the White House. Before the President arrived, Mrs. Eisenhower, with her customary gracious hospitality, was showing us around the living quarters. Pausing in one room, she told of a former home and how her husband would pace the floor at night sharing with God his burdens as General during World War II. She recalled one occasion when he called out, "Oh God, I haven't enough men, I haven't enough men." But after further conversation with his God, he finally said, "Goodnight, God, goodnight" and went to bed and slept like a baby.

Mrs. Eisenhower went on to say that as president, before going to sleep her husband would say his prayers and end with "God, I've done the best I could today." What quiet poise and power can possess a leader with such trust in the sovereignty of God!

On another occasion while I was in Washington, Secretary of State John Foster Dulles was sitting in church in front of the President at a Sunday morning service. Secretaries of state, like premiers and prime ministers of other lands, have been called the "whipping boys of history." In the decisions they must make, they are "damned if they do and damned if they don't" by the opinionated masses. As with a basketball referee, no matter what the call, some cry, "Throw him out." During the morning prayer, I prayed something like this, "Lord, bless our secretary of state. May he, amid all the praise and blame of public life, hear the drum-call of your will and your words: 'This is the way; lead them to it.' God give him courage." At the close of the service, as I was walking out of the church during the closing hymn, Secretary of State Dulles, standing at his pew seat on the aisle, reached out and took my hand in both of his and said hastily, "Thank you for that prayer, Dr. Evans—it's very difficult and lonely at times." To this I replied, "I am sure of that, sir. But when you are not alone, then it is all right isn't it?" And he answered, "Yes, then it is all right." Oh, the peace and power of the Presence of God.

A man who was calling on his farmer friend asked, "How is the family?" The farmer replied, "Oh, things are going quite well. Had a good crop. Hay's in the barn. Cattle doing well. But my wife, Maggie, though feeling quite well—no ague this time of year—is fine except for her worryin'. Maggie is just sure that Carolyn, who had diphtheria, just might not make it someday. And, Bill, he has to row across the river to work, and she's sure he's going to be drowned someday. Bob works in the big town now, and she is

afraid that he's going to 'stub his toe' one of
these days. You know, Maggie can trust God
with the whole world, but she just can't trust
God with the family." Can we?

May we dare personally to pray this prayer:
*"O God, find me worthy of enjoying your presence
when I pray. Through the surrender of my heart,
make me your child. May I stand before you par-
doned, may your will become mine. Give me trust
in your guidance. Then shall I have your ear because you have my heart. Then I shall know the
luxury of your presence. Amen."*

3.

SH! LISTEN!

Have You Learned How?

IN THE PREVIOUS CHAPTER, we were assured that God would hear us—under certain conditions—primarily if he is our "Father." Now the second question: Are we willing to listen to God? The answer is more easily assumed than it is performed.

God says, "If then I am a father, where is my honor?" (Mal. 1:6, RSV). If I go to my father with a problem and after giving my appraisal of it, I suggest my own possible solution and am up and gone without even allowing him to say a word and offer his own solution, I can hear him say to me, "Come back, son, and sit down. I thought you wanted my opinion and you have not given me a chance to say a word. Don't you want to know how Dad feels? Do you really have some respect for my opinion?" Did I really feel that what I had to say to my dad was more important than what he had to say to me?

Prayer is like this for many of us—we disrespectfully monopolize the conversation and do all the talking. Prayer should be a dialogue of give and take.

In one of my churches there was a certain woman who would call me often, usually in the mornings when I was trying to study. More than this, her conversation was so often about trivia—a lost article left in the church, a question that the secretary easily could have answered. Her voice was often like a "river of words with a trickle of mind." I am glad that she couldn't see me on occasions when I tucked the phone between my ear and shoulder and paid only partial attention as the situation justified it. I could not get a word in sideways. She monopolized the conversation. This may seem ill-bred and impolite. But so often this is how we talk to God.

A woman once said to my father, her pastor, "Dr. Evans, God has promised to answer prayer, but so often he gives me no answer. I'm worried." My father said, "And so is God. Be honest, now. Do you give him a chance to answer you? When you have said your say, made your request, do you remain silent and give him a chance to answer you? Which do you think is the more important—what you have to say to him or what he has to say to you? Have you learned to listen?" She queried, "But how do you listen?" It was evident she had never learned to do that. Many of us have the same problem. When we are finished with our chatter and wordy speaking, we feel the prayer is over, and we are up from our knees or out of our chair or have our ear tucked into the pillow, before God has a chance to reply.

Oliver Wendell Holmes must have been a harpist, for he said, "When you are playing a harp, part of the artistry is to not only thrum the strings, but to put your palm on them to silence their twanging." Part of the artistry of the pianist lies in the proper use of the soft pedal. The wise speaker knows the "power of the pause." It allows time for his message to sink in.

There ought to be pauses in our praying. There are two parts of ourselves that we must use in praying—our lips in speaking, our ears in listening. The latter are the more important.

My father came to the United States from England when he was nineteen years of age. While working for his Ph.D. at the University of Chicago, he decided, with normal student curiosity, to hear D. L. Moody who was then speaking in Chicago. He sat in the fourth row of the large auditorium. Suddenly, in the midst of the sermon, Moody paused, and pointing his finger at my father, said to him, "Young man, hasn't God called you to the ministry?" My father, a perfect stranger to Moody, made no response not being sure he was the target of the question. Impatiently Moody, pointing to him again, said, "You, young man sitting in that fourth row—hasn't God called you to the ministry?" Now my father had been struggling some with this urge and he mumbled, "Well, sir, I have been thinking about it." Moody said, "See me after the meeting, young man." My father tarried after the meeting and made an appointment to see Moody the next morning. When he called at the office, a young man asked, "Are you Mr. Will Evans?" He replied, "I am." "Will you please have a chair. Mr. Moody is expecting you, but he is at prayer just now." My father sat there and could hear Moody's voice lifted in a few earnest sentences—then silence—another earnest utterance—then ten long minutes of silence. This was repeated until nearly a half hour passed. Then my father was invited in. But in that time of waiting my father had discovered the secret of that giant evangelist's prayer power: Moody had talked to God for just seven minutes, but God had talked to Moody for twenty-three minutes. He had learned to listen! That was one reason Moody shook the world.

How afraid we are of silence in God's presence! When I was pastor in Hollywood, one of the women who was presiding at a session of one of our "prayer cells" said to me, "Dr. Evans

I must give up the leadership of my prayer group." When I asked why, she replied, "Well, I was so embarrassed yesterday—I suggested that anyone who felt led should lead in audible prayer. For about ten minutes no one said a word. I was so distressed I could have fallen through the floor. As a leader I am a failure—no one said a word!" I smiled and said, "Thank God, dear lady, that they were giving God a chance to say his word. That's our trouble. We have forgotten how to wait on God." The prophets, men of power, used to say, "Speak, Lord, thy servant heareth." We often merely say, "Listen, Lord, thy servant speaketh."

A businessman said to me regarding this condition, "You know, sir, the other day when I was praying I said to myself, 'Shut up!' It has changed my whole prayer life." It might do just as well to say to our loquacious, talkative selves, "Listen now."

But wait a moment. *How does one hear the voice of God?* Is it a definite audible voice? Some have claimed this. Moses heard God call him at the burning bush. Mary heard God's call at Nazareth. Paul heard that audible voice on the road to Damascus. Others have claimed this kind of experience today, but it is certainly not for all. God or the Holy Spirit could easily assume a human larynx; they created it.

Another way of giving God first chance to

speak is.to "*have the mind of Christ*" (see 1 Cor.
2:16, AMPLIFIED). This means that he is so con-
trolling your thought processes that when you
feel you are working out the problem yourself,
shaping your own answer, you have simply so
come to a knowledge of Christ—in your surrender to him, your fellowship and walk with him,
your spiritual thought-style, your obedience
and Christ-nearness, your study of his word—
that when you think you are working out the
answer for yourself, he is doing the thinking for
you, mastering your thought processes. And you
are enjoying the liberating control of the "mind
of Christ."

Then there is the *use of the Bible* as the
"springboard of prayer." This approach consists of reading a few verses quietly,
thoughtfully—not too many—and then stop-
ping to think about what God has been saying to
us in what we have read. This is giving him the
first chance to speak to us. Then we can talk to
him about what *he* has been saying in his Word.

In this way, the Holy Spirit will be taking us
by the hand and mind and leading us along the
paths of his thought processes. This will get us
out of the childish rut of "Now I lay me down to
sleep" or our adult version of it, and lead our
minds along the paths of his own choosing. That
delivers us from a dull devotional life.

Let us take care to *teach our children to listen.*

This is vital to their spiritual development. Read carefully 1 Samuel 3:1–10, RSV. Here the boy Samuel has been placed under the tutelage of Eli, the High Priest. During the night Samuel hears a voice saying, "Samuel, Samuel." Rushing to Eli he said, "Here I am, for you called me." Eli replied, "I did not call; lie down again." This happened three times and Eli, sensing that the Lord was calling to the lad, said to him, "Go, lie down; and if he calls you, you shall say, 'Speak, Lord, for thy servant hears.'"

There comes the time, parents, when children need to be trained rightly, to heed the voice of God in guiding prayer, rather than our own. It is a time when our authority must *decrease* while God's *increases*—a time when our human authority gradually yields to his heavenly, all-wise tutelage. God grant that we shall have schooled our children in this way. This may be hard on our "parental ego," but it is the right salute to the guidance of God in their lives. Will this glorious transfer of final authority be magnificently accomplished at our hearthsides when the proper time has come? "He who loves [reveres] father or mother more than me is not worthy of me" (Matt. 10:37, RSV). May their minds become gradually tuned in to the wavelength of the voice of God because we have taught them to listen to God and so to be led of the Spirit.

Learning to hear the voice of God or the revelation of his will to us is *going to take time.* Years
ago, before electricity was installed, we visited
the Mammoth Cave in Kentucky. Inside the
cave, we had to sit quietly in the dim light of
tapers. At first all was darkness. Then gradually
as our eyes grew accustomed to the dim light,
we began to see the white forms of those classic
stalagmites and stalactites as they became
flashing castles of beauty. But we had to wait!
You and I must not be hurried if we are to see the
plans and heart of God unfolding for us, in all
their majesty.

The trouble is that in praying many of us set
the cameras of our minds to "instantaneous"—
even the hundredth of a second. We might try to
survive on early morning devotions, cut off in
short telegram-style. Or, after an exhausting
day, we may generously read a few verses, yawn
in God's face, turn off the light and go to sleep.

John Ruskin once said, "You see the unseen
by an effort of the mind. To look at Jesus to be
present, as if in the body, at every recorded
moment of the history of the Redeemer, is hard
but it can be done if you practice it."

In the Holy Land, the streams of Shechem run
underneath the streets of the busy marketplace.
You cannot hear them for the noise of braying
donkeys, the moaning camels, and the noisy
voices haggling at the exchange. But if you will

wait until the crowd has gone home and the sun is setting, as you sit alone on the bench and listen, you will hear those deep streams of Shechem as they flow to meet the sea. You and I have to find some time away from the calling of the marketplace, the din of traffic, the clatter of the knitting loom, the cry of children, the laughter and noise of the classroom, and the mad panic of the stadium to find some place to be quiet—a place where we can hear God's expansive and perfect will for us.

Surrender of the will is another way to hear the voice of God. This often entails self-denial. In the old days of telephony, when the wires were still poorly insulated, we suffered from what was called the "power of induced current." When we expected to hear a certain voice, another voice from a neighboring wire would leap across and find its way along the adjacent wire. We were hearing the wrong voice. Many times we are not satisfactorily "insulated" from selfishness. Often when we expect and hope to hear the voice of God, we hear the voice of self taking over.

People will often go to the Bible and use it, twist it, and interpret it so as to make it concur with their own selfish interests. It is terrifying and amazing what some people can make the Bible say to meet their contention and confirm their prejudice. Proper Bible study entails

"*ex*egesis"—(*ex* in the Greek means "out of") to
get out of the passage what *God* has put into it.
For some, however, it is "*i*segesis"—to put into
or read into it what *I* desire it to say. The Scrip-
tures are often unfairly blamed when this mis-
carriage of truth is exercised.

When you pray, say "Lord." Only a *servant*
can call him *Lord.* "Why call ye me, Lord, Lord,
and do not the things which I say?" (Luke 6:46,
KJV). God is not willing to keep revealing his
will to those who will not follow it if they see it.
Why give a person a road map if he is not going
anywhere? Why should God reveal his will to us
if we will not do anything about it anyway?
With the mental curiosity of *wanting to know,*
there must also be the spiritual *willingness to
obey.*

One day a young man came to a well-known
clergyman in the East and was contemplating
doing something shockingly wrong. The pastor
was amazed that the young man would even
consult him about it. The pastor said to him,
"How do you feel when you pray about it?" He
replied, "Well, then it seems shockingly
wrong." The pastor said to the young man, "You
know, young man, the great thing about prayer
is that it strips the mask from the face of temptation; it reveals it for what it is, takes away its
respectability and its tricky pose. Prayer tears

away the disguise and reveals the hideous features. If it's wrong, young man, it can't stand the light. Prayer is bringing things into the light. If you want to see clearly and know the will of God, then ask." *It takes courage to ask.* God said to Israel, "Seek ye my face [look me in the eye]" (Ps. 27:8, RSV).

It was once said to Napoleon, "There is treason in your Old Guard, sir." He said, "I don't believe it, but I will find out." He had members of the Old Guard stand in the vestibule of the throne room. He himself sat on the throne. It was arranged that the guard should come one at a time and face the emperor. The door was opened, one of the guard entered the throne room and the door was shut behind him; he walked up the long carpeted aisle, stood before his emperor, looked him straight in the eyes—his gaze never flinching. Then the emperor put out his hand and held it as long as one man dare hold another's; the guard saluted, did a right-about-face and walked out of the throne room. The next guard did the same until every man had stood alone in the presence of his king. Later Napoleon said to the man who had accused his guards, "There is no treason in my guard—not one man dropped his eyes!" When we pray God says, "Seek my face—look me in the eye." When we talk about that troublesome thing, do we drop our eyes? Then give it up. "Whatsoever is not of faith is sin" (Rom. 14:23, KJV). Never mind the motley crowd.

We can often find out more about our personal mores and conduct and the right or wrong of it on our knees talking with God than with any pastor, psychiatrist, teacher, parent, or one who poses as a friend. This can often be the final check in the realm of conduct and ethic.

How dynamic and dependable this could be in our national and international affairs. When Lincoln was in Springfield, he was not much of a churchman nor did he have much of a creed. But when he came to Washington he said, "God, I cannot do this alone. I shall fail unless You help me." When a friend saw him rise from his knees, his eyes all bloodshot with praying, he said, "Lincoln, do you pray?" Crisply Lincoln replied, "Man, I'd be the most presumptuous blockhead on God's footstool if I thought I could run the affairs of this government for five minutes without asking God to show me how!" Pastor Gurley of the New York Presbyterian Church in Washington D.C. testifies to the faithful attendance of Lincoln at Sunday morning services and at mid-week prayer meetings. During those dangerous "abolition days" the secret service warned Lincoln against going out in the evenings without adequate security guards, but occasionally he used to throw his cape over his shoulders, steal into the pastor's study and with the door ajar, unseen by those inside, join in with the others in their songs and prayers. All the while in those days, through sermons, Bible reading, and prayers he was imbibing the truths of the fatherhood of God and the brotherhood of man.

One day there lay on his desk the as yet unsigned Emancipation Proclamation. Gazing at it he cried, "God, who am I that thou should ask this of me? If I sign this then thousands will hiss my name and curse the day of my birth!" The compass of conscience was now vascillating crazily between public opinion and political expediency and the right as God saw it. He did then what he often did—sank to his knees and said, "God, I am nothing, but truth is everything and I know equality is right because Christ teaches it and Christ is God! If there is a place for me to be offered, I am ready now." By his action he began the process to free and save a race—an action that also resulted in his death. The needle of his conscience had pointed straight to Jesus Christ—his "Magnetic North." For Lincoln, Christ stood above the crowd, his Master above the mob.

An American historian said that it was this triumvirate that brought about, in the main, this emancipation: Lincoln in the White House; Dr. Henry Ward Beecher, the abolitionist preacher, in his pulpit; Harriet Beecher Stowe, his sister, who wrote *Uncle Tom's Cabin*. It cost Lincoln his life to "listen," but he still lives in the hearts of a nation and a world.

I have no idea what it might cost you to say, "Speak, Lord, I am ready to listen and to act."

On one of my trips to Africa I visited the town of Lambaréné where Albert Schweitzer's hospital was located. I would like to share what Norman Cousins said about his visit to that hospital in his book *Dr. Schweitzer of Lambaréné*:

> At the end of dinner each evening at his jungle hospital in Lambaréné, French Equatorial Africa, Dr. Albert Schweitzer would fold his napkin, announce the number of the hymn to be sung, get up and walk over to the upright piano on the other side of the room. . . .
>
> I doubt whether I shall ever forget my shock and disbelief when, the first evening of my visit, I saw him approach the upright. . . . It must have been at least fifty years old. The keyboard was badly stained; double screws fastened the ivory to each key. . . . The volume pedal was stuck and the reverberations . . . hung in the air. One or more strings were missing on at least a dozen keys.
>
> Before coming to Lambaréné, I had heard that under equatorial conditions of extreme heat and moisture, one doesn't even try to keep a piano in tune. . . .
>
> . . . Here was one of history's greatest interpreters of Bach, a man who could fill any concert

hall in the world. The best grand piano ever made would be none too good for him. But he was now about to play a dilapidated upright virtually beyond repair. And he went at it with the dignity that never leaves him.

I knew then I would never be able to put out of my mind the image—painful in one sense, exalting in another—of Schweitzer at the old upright in Lambaréné. For here was the symbol, visible and complete, of everything he had given up in order to found a hospital in Africa. Renunciation by itself might mean little. What is renounced and the purpose of the renunciation— that is what is important. In the case of Albert Schweitzer, renunciation involved a distinguished career as organist and pianist.

... The amazing and wondrous thing was that the piano seemed to lose its poverty in his hands. Whatever its capacity was to yield music was now being fully realized. The tinniness and chattering echoes seemed subdued. It may be that this was the result of Schweitzer's intimate acquaintance with the piano, enabling him to avoid the rebellious keys and favor only the co-operative ones. Whatever the reason, his being at the piano strangely seemed to make it right.

When I read this account, I thought of some of us—redecorating our fine-looking houses that need redecorating as much as a man needs two heads, trading in our new cars every year just to keep up with the Joneses. Albert Schweitzer did

not even have an easy chair because the money
had to be spent on something else. When he sat
down, he leaned against the steel bedstead. But
here was a man that listened to God.

It is hard to preach in days like these. But the
minister's task is to put on the "earphones" and
listen to God and then tell the people what God
has said no matter what it might cost him. A
minister has just one person to please and that
is Jesus Christ. We must expect the pastor, like a
curator, a physician of souls, to be willing to cut
to cure and to hurt to heal. He was not called to
please us—but to heal us. Pray that God will
give him the courage.

The ministry of Christ is no place for sissies. A
contemporary theologian once said: "This is a
day in which you can get hurt if you talk like
Christ—even in the midst of Christendom."
Many a messenger of God has stood like the
martyr, St. Cyprian, pierced through with the
arrows fired sometimes from the bows of Christians.

Some might shun the ministry to avoid the
emotional stress. For example, a youth had been
missing church. "Haven't seen you lately," his
pastor commented. "How's your devotional
life?" He answered, "Not good, sir, I haven't
been wanting to talk to God lately. I'm afraid he
might call me into the ministry, and I just don't
want to don the clerical collar." "You're a cow-

ard, Howard," his pastor retorted. A month later the young man said to his pastor, "I talked with God about that, sir. He didn't want me in the ministry, but if he had, I would have been willing. I am at peace now—it's great to listen, sir, isn't it?"

If our answer to God's call has to do with anything that might have threatened our worth to him and his nearness to us—staying by a difficult marriage for the sake of a vow, the church, or the children; taking that committee responsibility, that Sunday school class, or choir membership (which can cut right across that desire to make Sunday only a play-day instead of the Lord's Day); making decisions of conscience and conduct; taking a promotion that threatens our spiritual image and aids compromise, any number of answers—then it must be weighed in the light of prayer.

In a high, beautiful mountain fastness in China, years ago a missionary conference program was coming to a close with a classic, warming solo. The young artist's soprano voice had all the sweetness of a birdsong and was clear as a bell. We listened spellbound as she stood there singing from that high rock under that moonlit sky. I whispered to one sitting near me, "What a voice! Who is she?" The answer came, "She was the soloist for the famous St. Olaf Choir. She was offered a position with a famous opera company after an audition, but she declined saying, "That is impossible. I have had another call." Christ had called her to China. After the program I asked her how it felt to turn her back on such possible fame and probable fortune. She warmly gave me her answer, "He needed me here." Why? The answer came in the song that welled up and echoed across the canyon:

> I know of a world that is sunk in shame
> Where hearts oft faint and tire;
> But I know of a Name, a precious Name
> That can set that world on fire.

Her voice had become that vital flame that was warming the souls of thousands in that faraway land. She had listened and obeyed.

It might help us to make this our occasional prayer: *"Oh God, my Father, whenever I pray, give me the courtesy to listen; give me courage to listen; give me the will to obey. Then I shall hear your voice because you have my heart. Amen."*

4.

FOR WHAT
SHALL WE PRAY?

The Majestic Sweep of Prayer

"ASK, AND IT WILL be given you" (Luke 11:9, RSV). For we know that "if we ask anything according to his will he hears us" (1 John 5:14, RSV). What is the legitimate sweep of prayer? Are we limiting it? Are we going too far? Are we asking too much or too little?

Already we have named some conditions of this requesting found in the Lord's Prayer: "Thy Kingdom come, Thy will be done, On earth as it is in heaven" (Matt. 6:10, RSV). We have already included "Give us this day our daily bread; and forgive us our debts . . ." (Matt. 6:11–12, RSV).

Now let's look at Christ's priestly prayer that he offered in the garden. What better possible outline for our asking could we have! As we note the various circles of his asking, we can set our pattern for our requests. (Read John 17.)

First of all, *he prayed for himself.* "Father, . . .

65

glorify thy Son that the Son may glorify thee"
(v. 1, RSV). Dare we begin with self? That depends. Note what he was asking for himself.
What does it mean to "glorify?" When you enter
an art gallery and the guide points out the excel-
lence and artistry of a painting or statue for
your appreciation and admiration, he is
"glorifying" that work. Christ was glorifying
the Father when he so lived, spoke, and felt that
one was moved to the admiration and worship
of his Father because they had "seen the Father"
in him. "He that hath seen me hath seen the
Father" (John 14:9, KJV). He must not fail lest
others lose faith in the Father. Here was an unselfish prayer for himself.

Likewise, we must pray an unselfish prayer
for ourselves that others may see God in our
lives. It is especially important for parents to
seek God's help in their task. If dads would
strive to be earthly expressions of God's own
ready forgiveness, providential care, and deep
concern, then there could be no better window
through which a child could see and understand
his heavenly Father than through the life of his
dad. This is why one father prayed this unselfish
prayer for himself:

> To feel his little hand in mine so clinging and so
> warm;

To know he thinks me strong enough to keep him
    from all harm,
To feel his little childlike trust in all that I can say
    or do—
It sort of shames a fellow, but it makes him better
    too;
And I reckon I'm a better man than what I used
    to be
Because I have this chap at home who thinks the
    world of me.
I wouldn't disappoint his trust for anything on
    earth,
Nor let him know how little I just actually am
    worth;
And after all it's easier that higher road to climb
With those little hands behind me to push me all
    the time;
And I reckon I'm a better man than what I used
    to be
Because I have this chap at home who thinks the
    world of me!

AUTHOR UNKNOWN

*"God, my Father, please don't let me stub my
toe! For his sake, Lord, keep me."* This is a dad's
unselfish prayer for himself.

God has feminine aspects, too. "As one whom
his mother comforts, so I will comfort you" (Isa.
66:13, RSV). In your understanding, your so-
licitude, your child sees God through you.

One mother found these lines on her desk, penned by her daughter:

> Oh Mother, when I think of thee
> 'Tis but a step to Calvary.
> Thy gentle hand upon my brow
> Is leading me to Jesus now.

Many of the young women who have won the Miss America title have used their prominence and honor for the glory of God. One told me that a line from Hebrews 11 was part of her devotions on the evening before the last and hardest day of testing. When she finished reading, she said to Christ, "Seeing then that we are surrounded by so great a cloud of witnesses if you wish me to have this honor, I pledge to use it for your glory." After winning the crown, she went about telling young women that beauty is more than skin deep—when feelings of guilt show through, physical beauty diminishes; but when love and beauty of soul shine through, the fresh goodness inside brightens the outward appearance. Another Miss America told me, "The greatest reward that this honor has bestowed on me is being able to serve Jesus Christ." Still another one said to a high school audience, "Remember, true beauty has less to do with curves and more with convictions." Is the glory we crave unselfishly motivated?

When we pray "Hallowed be thy name" we must remember that that name, which "we wear on our foreheads" must do honor to the One whose name we bear. We are God's labels or his libels.

Alexander the Great was riding along on his charger. Along the road he saw a man wearing the uniform of his army, but staggering along in a drunken stupor. Angrily commanding the soldier to halt, he said, "What is your name, sir?" "It's Alexander, sir," the soldier replied. "Don't trifle with me, I am asking you again, what is your name?" Again the soldier replied, "Honestly, sir, it is Alexander." Then the emperor said, "Then either change your name or your livery!"

How high on our asking list is our prayer for a Christlike *character?* Adolph Schlatter tells of a man who lay dying. His dear friend was comforting him with words like, "Have no fear. Soon heaven will be yours; you will be walking the golden streets, drinking from silver goblets, enjoying the mansions." The aged Christian exclaimed, "Away with that rubbish! All I want is to be like my Lord."

Our prayer-life has gone a long way when we make this our prime request—"Not *give me,* but *make me* like Thee, O God."

Christine Miller, an outstanding Christian character, had been one of the world's leading contraltos, making many Edison records. She was now the wife of D. M. Clemson, a high officer and millionaire partner of the Carnegie Steel Corporation and President of our church Board of Trustees. One Sunday after the morning service she said to me, "Pastor, do you think eternity will be long enough to make me like Jesus Christ?" I replied, "You would rather have that than anything else in the world, wouldn't you, Christine? Then you will be." Is that our highest request when we pray?

Intercessory prayer is our prayer for others. "I am praying for them" (John 17:9, RSV).

Two men were strolling across a hill. They came upon a large reservoir of water. They had been discussing the power of prayer that interceded for others. Said one, "In that reservoir there is a large volume of water—not all the water in the community but some. It has a certain density and life-giving, thirst-quenching characteristics. Pipes carry that water to different parts of our city: buildings, schools, farms, and homes."

Not all the available blessings of God are in the reservoir of intercessory prayer—but some are. Your prayers are the pipes which direct those blessings to that hospital room of that dear one; to that dormitory room where your son or daughter lives; to that kitchen where your wife is at work; to that public fountain where the thirsty go. God is pleased to use the pipes of our prayers in the blessing of others.

In intercessory prayer we are not the *recipients* of the blessings so much as the *channels* of those blessings.

Robert Milliken was a weekend guest at our home during one of my pastorates. He was one of the world's greatest physicists, a Nobel-prize-winner in geophysics, and an elder in the church. He spoke of two kinds of light. One is the ordinary light of the sun that shines with its rising and goes down with its setting. The other is the type of light that is called the "cosmic ray." This light is continually radiating, giving off light night and day, winter and summer, spring and fall. All you have to do to avail yourself of it is to be alive. What is it? It comes from the great stellar spaces—not from any one star. It comes from one united cosmic orchestration of suns losing themselves and uniting themselves to give light.

So must we of God's kingdom unite to shed the cosmic orchestration of all our hearts and prayers for the entire world, for those whom we know and love and those, whom having not seen, we still love. This is the power of collective prayer.

Christ prayed for the *Inner Circle:* "I pray for them ... which thou hast given me" (John 17:9, KJV).

What are our most ardent requests for those in *our family circle?* David prayed, "Give unto Solomon my son a perfect heart" (1 Chron. 29:19, KJV). Not popularity, power, position— but purity of heart and motive. Solomon later, when asked what his most ardent desire might be, said in essence, "Thou rememberest my father, David: Give me a double portion of his spirit." I want to be like my dad! What a tribute from a son.

A mother, though widowed, was so successful with her two daughters and five sons that she was asked the secret. This was her answer: "When I made them ready in the morning I prayed this prayer: 'As I wash them—*cleanse them in thy love;* as I give them bread—*feed them on the bread of life;* as I put on their garments— *clothe them in thy righteousness;* as I send them off to school—*teach them my God, thy Truth;* as I love them—*love them more, most Holy Father.'*" Prayer had sealed her success.

Prayer for the church. "I pray not that thou shouldest take them out of the world, but that thou shouldest keep them from the evil. They are not of the world, even as I am not of the world" (John 17:15–16, KJV). The world here stands for compromise, pride, lust, coveting.

The church is in the world but the "world" must not get into the church. A bottle may float on the water, but when the water gets in the bottle, then it sinks. A fly may rest on the water, but let the water soak its wings and it is captured. Let it keep its wings dry and it flies to freedom.

There are some who say that to be successful in this contemporary age, the world must be allowed to change the message of the church; but the need today is that its message change the world. The diamond must cut the glass, not the glass cut the diamond.

Many of the early church possessed that certain uniqueness of behavior and courage that easily identified them. Saul was on his way to Damascus to take captive the people "of The Way." They had a way about them—they stood out like a tall Mt. Olympus in the midst of the low straggling foothills of a decaying Roman ethos. Christ had reminded them that a light placed on a candlestick could not be hidden. This is a captivating facet of the church's success: it maintains its light.

Someone asked Dr. Spurgeon why his church was crowded every Sunday. He replied, "I preach the gospel on Sunday and my people live it out all week." That can prove to be convincing and attractive to those who insist on judging belief by behavior!

Christ prayed for the *unity of the church:* "I ... pray for ... those who believe in me through [the] word *that they may all be one"*

(John 17:20–21, RSV). This does not mean that the churches must all be uniform. One can have unity of spirit without union of organization. Admit there are too many divisions in the church, but admit that in the Body of Christ, which is the church, there can be many members of that body. I have ten fingers, but they are all my fingers—guided by a single mind, but each differing somewhat from the other. Were all the fingers welded into one, I might have a clumsy mitten less adapted to some of the functions demanded of a group of coordinating but separate fingers. The tragedy would be if the fingers on my right hand should reach over and tear off, like a savage, the fingers of my left hand, belonging to the same body; that would be self-mutilation. Like the wild man of Gadara who was tearing himself to pieces self-mutilation within the church would indicate madness—failure to rightly discern the body of Christ.

Let us remember our inherent oneness. "As many as received Him, to them He gave the right to become children of God." (John 1:12, NKJV). Then as many as call God "Father" must of necessity address each other as "brother" and "sister." This does not mean exact agreement on all issues of faith and conduct. We must be "brothers" and "sisters," but not necessarily "identical twins." Many Christians around the world are thanking God for a newer and deeper ecumenicity and oneness that in its deeper sense spells unity without uniformity.

Prayer for the ministers will have its place on the list of intercessions. Paul keeps asking the Ephesian church to pray for him that he may speak *with boldness.* "[Pray] ... for me, ... that I may open my mouth *boldly,* to make known the mystery of the gospel, For which I am an ambassador in bonds: that therein I may speak *boldly,* as I ought to speak" (Eph. 6:18–20, KJV).

Preaching the gospel with boldness takes courage. Christ spoke boldly and they crucified him; John the Baptist preached it and they beheaded him; the same thing befell Paul; Peter spoke out and died head downward on a cross; Matthew preached it and they ran him through with a lance; thousands die for Christ each year in our own time. But courage lives on, and the "blood of the martyrs becomes the seed of the church." Pray then for the minister that he might have the courage to speak God's Word boldly—pray for a daring and a vital witness in a compromising world.

Pray for world missions. "I ... pray ... for those who believe in me through their word, ... that the world may believe that thou hast sent me" (John 17:20–21, RSV). Let your mission prayer book be a partner to your Bible. I have been deeply impressed, as I have visited a dozen mission fields abroad, to learn how new life and courage and a sense of belonging wells up in the hearts of missionaries when they know by the printed mission prayer calendar that on a certain day, the arms of thousands of Christians around the world are about them in prayer from morn till night. As Alfred, Lord Tennyson wrote in *Idylls of the Kings*, "More things are wrought by prayer than this world dreams of.... For so the whole round earth is every way bound by gold chains about the feet of God."

Pray for your nation. Paul cried out to God, "My ... prayer to God for Israel is, that they might be saved" (Rom. 10:1, KJV). Christ besought God for those who dwelt in the capitol of his nation. "O Jerusalem, ... How often would I have gathered your children together as a hen gathers her brood under her wings and you would not!" (Luke 13:34, RSV).

Let us take care as to *what our prayers covet for our land.* Pray not simply that she be held as God's darling in his everlasting arms, but that America be held as an instrument of rightness and love in the hand of God—feared by those who do evil, loved by those who do good. "America First" to be sure—but in love and justice, in mercy and goodness—bending like a gentle giant over a weak and stricken world like a Good Samaritan. Only that nation that would *save* is worth saving.

Pray for your enemies. "Pray for them which despitefully use you, and persecute you" (Matt. 5:44, KJV). Be like a living tree which, when smitten with the axe, covers the vicious blade with the sweet sap of forgiveness.

Here is a challenge: Place at the head of your prayer list tonight the name of the one you deem to be your worst enemy. See how prayer lances the pus sacs of hatred and drains them dry. You cannot go on hating those for whom you sincerely pray.

Years ago when Mr. Khrushchev was a guest of honor of the chancellor of the University of Pittsburgh, the university was warned that prayer at the table might offend the Russian guest. The chancellor let it be known that grace was said at the university's tables and even though it might offend the guest, he preferred not to offend God. All the while Dr. Scarfe, pastor of a Pittsburgh church was saying the grace, Khrushchev's interpreter was whispering every translated word into the Russian leader's ear. At the conclusion of the prayer Mr. Khrushchev thanked Dr. Scarfe for his words. Mrs. Khrushchev said after the luncheon that she would appreciate a copy of that prayer so that she might take it home to Russia with her. "Careful now," some might say. "It might be a sly pose and meaningless gesture." It might have been—but perhaps not. Dare we forget the truth so clearly stated in these lines from a hymn by Fanny J. Crosby, "Down in the human heart, Crush'd by the tempter, Feelings lie buried that grace can restore; Touch'd by a loving heart, Waken'd by kindness, Chords that are broken will vibrate once more"?

At an airport many years ago, a man told me that he had just returned from Russia and had information that Mrs. Khrushchev had embraced Christianity and that her influence on her husband had been so ameliorating that his hatred became lacking. He was willing to live in a co-prosperity sphere so he was ousted.

Why did Joseph Stalin's daughter make her way from his pagan hearthside to this land of ours? Was it that here a heart could more easily find the way to the heart of God? God knows, whether we know or not.

As someone has said, "The prayer of faith is the awareness of a power that can be used because it can be as strong as God himself."

Shall we make this our prayer? *O God, give me all the luxury of the great, loving sweep of prayer: for the harmless babe whom I love to the most formidable, unruly monarch of the world; from the intimate hearthside that I love to the far corners of the earth; may we dare thee, mighty God, to do daring things and never insult thee by timid asking.*

Lord, teach us to pray. Through Christ, amen.

5.

WHY UNANSWERED PRAYERS?

Do We Want HIS Answer?
Do We Ask Amiss?

LOVING GOD, WE thrill at your promise, "If you call, I will answer." Then your answer, "You ask and do not receive, because you *ask amiss.*" (James 4:3, NKJV). What is wrong—where do we miss the mark? If our bank is in good condition and our account also, the check, if properly signed, should go through. If it does not we should inquire of the banker. If there is sufficient water in the city's reservoir and at the turn of our tap no water flows, we call the plumber. If the car has power and yet is stalled, something is wrong—ignition, fuel, the starter. Then we take it to the garage. If our prayer life loses its power, we bring it to the church and ask honestly with concern, "What is amiss?"

Perhaps our desires are too materialistic. "A man's life consisteth not in the abundance of *things* which he possesseth" (Luke 12:15, KJV). But are not things important, necessary? We ask, "Give us this day our daily bread." We must eat. Heavenly Father, you know this battle for bread, this fierce competition in the marketplace—the unemployment, the crop failures, the sometimes fruitless toil. But perhaps we have made *things* our first love. Our primitive, pagan wishes are normally for *things*. "The Masai of Africa," said one missionary, "pray every morning, 'God of my distress, give me food, give me milk, give me children, give me meat.'" Gimme, gimme, gimme!

God knows we have need of these things—and we also should be concerned that others have the necessities of life. These necessities enable us to make a living. But are we aware of what we are living for? Are we *making a life?* Remember, "a man's life consists not [alone] in the abundance of things that he possesseth" (Luke 12:15, KJV). Christ teaches us to "seek *first* the Kingdom of God and His righteousness, and all these things will be added" (Matt. 6:33, NKJV). It is not just a matter of what money you are making, but what your money is making of you; your character is more than cash—it is your greatest gift to God and to the world. As far as we know Christ had no bank account, owned no real estate; so far as we know, he did not own his own home; he lived on meager fare and at the last had one thing he owned—his coat—and at the cross they threw dice for that! Yet, no man gave as he gave; none is so loved as he—he gave his life.

It must please God that while needfully asking him for things, we also come thanking him for himself and for his love for us and naming our love for him. One Sufi woman of India, running with a torch in one hand and a pail of water in the other, prayed, "I want to burn up heaven with the torch and put out the fires of hell with the water, and then we will not love God for the hope of reward in heaven or of escaping fire in hell—we will love him just for himself." Do we ever go to him, not to ask for anything save to be with him and to thank him for his love—not incessantly asking for his presents, but just for his presence? Do we ever say, "This time I have nothing to ask for—I just desire the luxury of your presence: there my soul delights to hide!"

Some prayers go unanswered because of *a selfish conflict of desires.* In the Fellowship of Christian Athletes, we have often discussed the unfairness of God giving our own team the victory when the man quarterbacking the opposing team, a Christian, might be asking or desiring the same thing. Have we the right to ask Christ to sit on a certain side of the football field in our own rooting section? Would not a prayer for victory in our own lives and characters be more proper? "God, help me to do my best, to take victory without conceit and defeat

without bitterness." Making men is of more
interest than making touchdowns, runs, points.
When I asked the farmers in my first church in
North Dakota if they could all agree on what
weather they desired the following week, I soon
found it was impossible! One wanted rain for
his newly planted winter wheat. Another
wanted sun to dry out his new-mown hay—he
had to get it in the barn. What was God to do?
Nations, of course, have the same problem. For
example, one French soldier said that he had a
vision in which he saw Christ standing with the
sword of France in his hand. But how embarras-
sing when a German wore on his belt buckle,
"*Gott mit uns*" ("God with us").

The basic test of our petitioning ought to be,
"Do we have in our minds and on our hearts the
supreme desire—'Thy kingdom come, *Thy will
be done*'?" It is hard to pray, "Put into office
that one who can best serve You and the city
and the nation" or "May election to office, promotion in the company or the society go to the
one who can best aid Your cause and ours."

General Stonewall Jackson, a great Christian
general in the Civil War, made this generous
petition to God, "O God, may this war soon be
over and *may the right side win* so that we may
return to our main task of winning men to Your
Kingdom." This he prayed in spite of military
humiliation and defeat. The success of our

prayers may often rest in the selflessness of
them. Warning: "Seekest thou great things for
thyself?"

*God sometimes displaces our plans to answer
with his own.* It is so easy to go to God with a
request that is a mandatory blueprint drawn up
by us, only reluctantly allowing him to red-
pencil or change the plan. We expect him to answer in a certain manner. But God changes *his
manner* of answering at times.

Augustine in his *Confessions* relates how his
mother was very desirous that he remain in
Carthage with her amid the spiritual surround-
ings that had tutored him. Restlessly he had
talked of going to Rome someday, but against
this plan she prayed fervently, "Not to Rome
with its paganism and godlessness!" Augustine
deceived her when one day a friend bound for
Rome was moored at the port of Carthage. She
was suspicious and offered to go down with him
to the port. He demurred, saying that she should
not expose herself to the coarse talk and de-
meanor of the stevedores and suggested she go
and pray at the Chapel of St. Cyprian. This she
did and while she was on her knees the ship
sailed for Rome—and Augustine was aboard!
His departure, contrary to her wish and her
wisdom, seemed to Monica a refusal of God to
answer her prayer. But while in Rome Augustine, walking by a monastary wall, heard the

voice of Ambrose reading the Scripture beyond the wall, and there he gave his heart and life to Christ. The denial of a mother's prayer was *God's way* of answering.

Of all this Augustine feelingly wrote, "But Thou in Thy hidden wisdom didst give the substance of her desire, yet refused the things she prayed for in order that Thou mightest effect in me what she was ever praying for. . . . She loved to keep me near her as mothers are wont, yes, far more than some mothers, and she knew not what joy Thou was preparing for her out of my desertion." William Cowper in his "Olney Hymns" wrote: "God moves in a mysterious way His wonders to perform." Be sure you have the right *motive* when you pray, but leave the *method* of answer to God. If we are in his will, we may not receive what we ask for, but we will receive what we should have asked for. His wisdom and love will work that out.

A very successful doctor friend of mine was stricken with tuberculosis. It meant the collapse of his plans, deserting his profession and home and moving to a far-off mountain fastness his doctor had prescribed. But there he began to treat a few patients; his expertise and following grew until he headed the great tuberculosis sanitarium where thousands have sustained life and found hope. God answered his prayer, but He chose His own scene for the answer. Scripture tells us that our ways are not God's ways (Isa. 55:8).

Some prayers seem to remain unanswered *because of our lack of cooperation.* God desires that we become a partner with him in the cause of our answered prayer by accepting our need of him. Christ is the vine and we are the branches, and as branches we cannot bear fruit unless we abide in the Vine. (See John 15:4–5). We bow to this. But do we accept the fact that neither can the vine bear fruit without the branches—and we are the branches? It is with some awe that we hear God say to us, "Your Lord has need of *you.*" What an honor to help God work out the answer! Blaise Pascal, the great scientist, once said, "Prayer is God's way of adding dignity to human life by involving man in causality." When some prayers are answered it is because God wished to involve us in the answer.

Prayer is not a substitute for work—it is an urge to work. When we ask that the world be fed, are we willing to do our part in the process? A boy heard his farmer-father pray fervently, "O God, feed the starving of the world." The lad, conscious of the family barns filled to overflowing, commented feelingly, "Gee, Dad, I wish I had your corn."

"Why do you say that, Son?"

"Because then I would answer your prayer with it."

Why don't we feed the starving ourselves? Our society sometimes has such an overabundance that we dump out thousands and thousands of bushels of wheat along the roadside, store up immense unused supplies, and even pay farmers for allowing their fields to lie useless while one half of India goes to bed hungry every night, and people are starving in Bangladesh. How easy it is to let complicated politics and excuses strangle our efforts or excuse our lack of love!

If prayers were a substitute for working, we would be committing intellectual suicide. A girl in her evening prayer said, "O God, please make Rome the capital of Turkey." Her bewildered mother said, "What made you ask that, dear?" The girl replied, "Well, Mother, that's the way I put it on my examination paper." Lazy study habits cannot plead for miracles in geography. Instead, prayer is an *urge* to work.

Some farmers, where I was a pastor, would not rotate their crops. They continued to plant wheat because it was easily disked in and spared them the rigors of growing other crops more suited to that climate. When some complained about the climate, I said, "Why ask God to change the climate when you could change your crops?" Let us not ask God to grow oranges in Alaska, to ripen apples where there is no frost, or to try to grow peaches where the freezes are frequent.

How difficult we make it for Deity, even with *our prayers for peace!* Instead of sitting down, when possible, and talking it out, we prefer often to fight it out. There are times when the sword is used in just defense. But how often are we too impatient to use arbitration? How often do we find it easier to resort to arms? How often do we blame God for our failures? For example, there is the sergeant who asked for volunteers to crawl across no-man's-land and spy on the enemy trenches. When the volunteers were halfway across the span, a star shell burst, and they were seen rushing to the refuge of a clump of dry bushes. In the swift enemy gunfire the bushes burst into flame. The sergeant shouted, "God, if you're going to roast them alive—do it fast!" To this outburst the chaplain nearby countered, "Shut up, Sarge. God didn't start that fire—we did."

It's a natural law that fire burns—do we want God to change his laws, or do we want to ask him to help us alter our ways? We scientifically make sure of the bomb-sight, aim it at the life beneath, and then pray to God to defy the law of gravity, defy combustion, and spare our sons. Even our prayers dare him to defy his laws which we misuse.

In the same vein, we expect things of our children which we are not willing to do ourselves. A mother, almost in tears, called me on the phone and said, "I was down at the military base as my son was leaving on liberty and the drunkeness I saw was deplorable. How can I keep my son from becoming a habitual drinker?" I said, "Do you drink?" Her answer was, "I do." I replied, "I don't think there is anything you can do. How can you fairly ask your son not to do what you insist on doing? All you can do is pray for him, and set him a better example."

Now and then a concerned father will say to me, "Can't you do something to get my son interested in God and church? Don't let him know I sicked you on to this—just tactfully get in your own word, will you?" In a case like that I always ask, "Do you go yourself?" If he says he does, I always say there is a good chance I can help. But if he says, "No," I usually reply, "I don't think we have a chance to win him." When he asks why, I say, "Because a boy once said to me, 'I don't want a God my dad doesn't need.' If you don't need God, then your son will think he has no need of him either." Parents, don't *send* your children to church, *bring* them. Our children need fewer critics and more examples.

My brother, Paul, would not mind my using this illustration. He was climbing fast in the business world. He had become the manager of a popular furniture store, a very demanding job which required expertise and sympathy. Rugged market problems added to the pressure. To relax, he frequently hunted on Sundays in that great "Temple of Nature" as some call it. One Sunday when he was out rabbit hunting with his son he sat down in the partial shade of a desert tree. It was 11:00 A.M. and the desert sun was merciless. He crossed his Levied legs, placed his gun across his knees with his sombrero lying across the gun, leaned his head back against a tree and slept. He awakened in a few minutes and looked across to where his son was resting. He, too, was leaning against a tree, booted Levied legs crossed, BB gun across his knees, and his sombrero across the gun—just like Dad. Paul stared at him and finally said, "All right, God—I see it—I get it!" Now he is a "regular" at church, an elder, and so is his son.

Prayers for the salvation of others are sometimes delayed for lack of our own witness. A churchman prayed ardently at a midweek service for the salvation of a friend, "O Holy Spirit, put your finger on him, put your finger on him." A friend sitting next to him whispered, "Why don't you put your own finger on him?" God has no lips but our own. We are his fingers, his hands, his lips.

Prayer for the world mission—the church is first of all a missionary society. In the syllabus to its laymen, the Presbyterian Church says: "The chief aim of the Church is the confrontation of all humanity with Jesus Christ as the Son of God and His program." Missions, then, is fundamental in the heart and purpose of the church—not something peculiar to a few people. When Christ said, "Go ye into all the world, and preach the gospel to every creature" (Mark 16:15, KJV), he was not addressing an anointed few—he was commanding all of us. And we must go in some way—whether it's in person, by financial support, or in our prayers.

E. Stanley Jones, as a young man, fastened a map of the world to the ceiling above his bed. Each night he asked God to bless the world and to send His messengers to specific areas. Eventually, Stanley himself went to India. Pray that God sends workers into his vineyard, and pray that you and your children be alert to God's calling—whatever it may be. World mission is having a struggle, but some of the results are breathtaking and encouraging.

After a trip to some twelve nations, I understand what Dr. Kenneth Latourette of Yale meant when, seeing the resurgence of mission in many nations, he said, "In a day when, at home, some churches are lagging in giving, sagging in membership, Christianity as a world movement has never seen a better day!"

May our prayers be crowned with such a sense of responsibility that we respond to the call so eloquently stated by Mary Ann Thompson:

Give of thy *sons* to bear the message glorious;
Give of thy *wealth* to speed them on their way;
Pour out thy soul for them in *pray'r* victorious;
And all thou spendest Jesus will repay.

It may cost you a great deal to answer your prayer for missions.

At the close of a missionary sermon, a woman of considerable wealth tarried after the service and said to the minister, "I heard what you said about those Korean refugees, who fleeing with five remaining sacks of grain, decided to give three of them to help build the mission chapel for their people. It made me ask what the mission of Christ was costing me." Quietly she removed the glove from her *right* hand and slipped a large diamond ring from her finger (clearly she could afford two rings) and placed it in her pastor's hand. "I think they need this more than I need it. You can get about three thousand dollars for this stone. It's the dearest thing I have—outside of His kingdom."

Our oldest daughter Lauralil's own small daughter once came to her mother and queried her about the price of a Bible. She learned it would take her entire savings of six dollars in carefully stacked coins and scanty bills. She wanted the Bible, not for herself, but for her friend, Rita. After deciding to make the purchase, Lauralil asked if she would like Rita's name put on it. Here is her answer as it appears in Laura M. Evans' book, *Hand in Hand: Mother, Child & God:*

> "Yes. In gold in the corner. Gold is pretty on white and then it will be really hers."
> "I'm sure she'll be very proud of it. And I am very proud of you. I think you are a very nice kind of daughter and I think the angel on your shoulder is smiling now".... Oh Rita, Rita, will you ever know what this gift cost this child? How long since I have loved so completely and cared so much for someone—or believed in the importance of God to this absolute limit?

The answer to *your prayer power* for the advancement of your claimed greatest task—the furtherance of the Kingdom of Christ on earth—might lie somewhere between the three-thousand-dollar gift and the six-dollar gift.

Idols in the heart can block the answer to prayer, "These men have set up their idols in their heart, and put the stumblingblock of their iniquity before their face: should I be enquired of at all by them?" (Ezek. 14:3, KJV). An idol is anything, anyone that comes between us and God. Often before we pray or as first we pray, we have to face up to those things displeasing to

God—things to which we cling more steadfastly than to God.

My father brought out this truth when, in conversation with a student, the young man admitted the collapse of his prayer and devotional life. He would not confess the blockage as yet, and his prayer life stalled. But one day it happened. My father, during his lecture, saw this young man lean against a window ledge (for the auditorium was quite crowded) and furtively strike a safety match beneath a small photograph he had taken from his wallet, set fire to it, and hold it in his hand until the flame had consumed the picture and was burning his fingers. As the ashes fell to the floor, the young man looked up to God and smiled. His idol had been a companionship that never should have been; now it was gone, and he could smile at God and God could smile at him. He and his heavenly Father could converse freely now. We all need to be able to honestly say:

> The dearest idol I have known, whate'er
>   that idol be,
> Help me to tear it from its throne and
>   worship only Thee.

Unforgiveness can block the answer to prayer. "Whenever you stand praying, forgive, if you have anything against any one; so that your Father also who is in heaven may forgive you your trespasses" (Mark 11:25, RSV). "Leave your gift . . . before the altar and go; first be reconciled to your brother, and then come and offer your gift" (Matt. 5:24, RSV). We block our forgiveness when we refuse to forgive another or ask the other's forgiveness of us.

At a session meeting, the pastor called upon a certain elder to lead in prayer. The elder said, "I am not ready to pray just yet—give me a moment, please." He stepped across the room, took the hand of another fellow elder and confessed, "I have been stabbing you in the back, my friend—and turned the knife as well. I am deeply sorry and ask your forgiveness. Grant me this." The other elder, somewhat taken aback, said, "And I have done the same in kind to you, sir. I am deeply sorry."

There were several exchanged contritions that night, and uncustomary praise exchanged between some hearts that had been cold before. After nearly two hours of this "agape" love-feast the pastor felt it was time to adjourn. He said to the clerk of session, "Well, I guess there is no business to report in the minutes for this evening." To this the clerk replied, "I have just recorded this in the session minutes: 'More was accomplished at this session tonight than ever before in the history of this church. We all fell in

love with each other afresh.' " It takes a forgiv-
ing love to make our prayers *work;* without it
our prayers are just *empty words.*

But our human hearts parry with, "But I was
the offended one; let the offender come first to
me." Not so with God! "God shows his love for
us in that *while we were yet sinners* Christ died
for us" (Rom. 5:8, RSV). He could have said, "I
will wait till they come to me." They both took
the initiative, "God gave his only son; the Son
gave himself." It was left for us to respond—we
who had sinned. The wounded Ones had come
first to the wounder! Do we?

When facing seemingly unanswered prayers,
God, give us the faith to believe that while we
may not get everything we asked for, we will get
everything we *should* have asked for. In the
midst of our disappointments, we need the trust
that changes one letter from a "D" to an "H":

To this end may I suggest this prayer:

> *Disappointment—His appointment*
> *Lord I take it then as such,*
> *Like the clay in hands of potter*
> *Yielding wholly to Thy touch.*
> *All my life's plan in Thy molding;*
> *Not one single choice be mine;*
> *Let me answer unrepining*
> *"Father, not my will but Thine."*
> *—Author Unknown*

6.

PRAYER AND THE HOME

Love, Marriage, and the Hearthside

THE HOME IS THE first institution God founded. He said, "It is not good that the man should be alone; I will make him an help meet for him" (Gen. 2:18, KJV).

If religion works anywhere it must work in the home. Home is also *the workshop of prayer.* It is this privilege and power of prayer that differentiates us from the animal kingdom. Prayer makes the home a domicile—not a den.

There should be a difference between a young colt scampering in the pasture on Sunday morning with his sire and a son worshiping with his father in God's house; between a sow suckling her piglet and the mother humming a hymn to the child at her breast; between the bear cuffing his cubs in discipline and a father explaining the laws of God to a child; between the way a dog gulps his food with no word, but a wagging tail, and the person who bows his head in thankfulness for his food.

A boy, visiting his friend for dinner, noticed that evidently no thanks were to be given for the meal and quietly exclaimed—"Gee, like my dog you start right in, too, don't you?" Do you and I? There ought to be a lot of difference between a farmyard and a fireside of faith. We must not neglect spiritual development in our households. As someone said, "If home is just a place of fleshly indulgence where we find folks acting relatively sweet or being at least moderately easy to get along with, and adequate clothing in the wardrobe and a little money in the bank, then that home could easily become stale and meaningless."

Let prayer prepare us for marriage. If God has established marriage for the welfare and happiness of mankind; if he invented the institution, then let him also be the engineer. Let God be a *partner in the choice of a life partner.* A collegian noticed that his roommate was spending extra time at prayer one evening. He said, "That took a long time. What were you talking to God about?" His friend answered, "I was asking him about my engagement." "What!" exclaimed the friend. "Do you bother God about that?" To this the other replied, "You know, Bud, I have three great choices to make in my life: one is the choice of a God—I have done that; then there is

the choice of a career—a life calling, I think I
have done that; then there is the choice of a life
partner, and that will have a lot to do with making my life a song or a sigh. It can make it or
break it."

I note that of late a lot of youth are thinking
about these choices. One young man said earnestly, "You know, I am giving a lot of thought
to this marriage business and my future partner;
I have seen that a careless 'puppy love' in high
school or college can lead to a 'dog's life' later
on." Smart talk that is!

Do not trust Dan Cupid. With his little bow
and arrow, he is not an adequate judge of partner choices. When he says to you, "Oh just put
your finger on your pulse, and if it's pounding go
ahead—it's love," what a little liar he is! A
young man came to me one day, all excited;
speaking breathlessly, he said, "You know, she's
lovely. Those eyes, sir—like deep pools—her
cheeks and that face—that voice!" He was pant-
ing like a lizard on a rock. You know what they
call that—adolescent, cardiac, respiratory
attack—and it can kill you after awhile! They
say "you can tell a man in love, but you can't tell
him much." But he listened. We talked about
not just falling in love, but about *walking into
love with your eyes open,* your minds asking
questions and the two of you asking each other:
"What are we living for?" Two cannot walk to-

gether unless they be agreed. Have you prayed it over together—talked to God about it together? Some say, "But that can come after marriage." If you cannot do it now, then what makes you think you can do it later? Let God help you two *think* it through now—not just *feel* it through.

Many churches are having classes on preparing for marriage. We had such a course, and I saw it work. It is surprising today how many young people and older people enter into this hoped-for, life-long involvement without knowing how God feels about it; and without knowing its demands, its meaning, and the things which make it abide.

Parents, you cannot make that choice for your children, but you can give them principles of choice. Often in a time like this, Mother and Dad—if wise, informed, firm and fair—can prove to be a tremendous aid and influence. Sometimes, at this stage, a pound of Christian dad can be worth a ton of parson, and a pound of Christian mother can be worth a ton of teacher or psychologist—though all these have their place. But *talk to God* about your choices.

At the request of my publisher, I would like to share with you my marriage prayer as it was recorded on Word Records' "Love, Marriage, and God" (W–3117):*

*"A Marriage Prayer" copyright © 1968 by Louis H. Evans, Sr.

A MARRIAGE PRAYER

O God of love, Thou hast established marriage for the welfare and happiness of mankind. Thine was the plan and only with Thee can we work it out with joy. Thou hast said, "It is not good for man to be alone. I have made a helpmeet for him." Now our joys are doubled since the happiness of one is the happiness of the other. Our burdens now are halved since when we share them we divide the load.

Bless this husband, bless him as provider of provender and raiment, and sustain him in all the exactions and pressures of his battle for bread. May his strength be her protection; his character be her boast and her pride; and may he so live that she may find in him the haven for which the heart of a woman truly longs. May his soul be so wide a sea that she may launch her all on its strong tide.

Bless this loving wife; give her a tenderness that makes her great, a deep sense of understanding and a great faith in Thee. Give her that inner beauty of soul that never fades, that eternal youth that is found in holding fast to the things that never age. May she so live that he may be pleased to reverence at the shrine of her heart.

May they never make the mistake of merely living for each other. Teach them that marriage is not [only] living for each other; it is two uniting and joining hands to serve Thee. Give them a great spiritual purpose in life. May they seek first the Kingdom of God and His righteousness, then the other things shall be added unto them. Loving Thee best, they shall love each other the more, and faithful unto Thee—faithful to each other they will be. May they not expect that perfection of each other that belongeth alone to Thee. May they minimize each other's weaknesses, be swift to praise and magnify each other's points of comeliness and strength, and see each other through a lover's kind and patient eyes. Give them a little something to forgive each day that they may grow in the graces of longsuffering and of love.

May they be as forebearing with each other's omissions and commissions as Thou art with theirs.

Now make such assignments to them on the scroll of Thy Will as will bless them and develop their characters as they walk together. Give them enough tears to keep them tender; enough hurts to keep them humane; enough failure to keep their hands clenched tightly in Thine; enough of success to make them sure they walk with God.

May they never take each other's love for granted but always experience that breathless wonder that exclaims, "Out of all this world you have chosen me."

Then when life is done and the sun is setting, may they be found then as now still hand in hand, still very proud, still thanking God so much for each other. May they serve Thee happily, faithfully, together, until at last one shall lay the other in God's arms.

This we ask through Jesus Christ, great lover of our souls. Amen.

Prayer right after marriage is of vast importance too. The values and habits which find their way into your home in the first five years are there to stay; what does not make its entrance then will have a hard time coming in later on. Start out as voyagers with Christ as your pilot, with his hand on the rudder, with his Word as your compass. This kind of beginning can do more than anything else to keep you off the rocks.

Mary and Paul are one young couple who began their marriage this way. Paul explained, "We began our living together in prayer—audible prayer. After we read the Bible, we knelt and I offered petitions for our home and especially that God would bless my Mary and make me a thoughtful husband. When I finished my prayer, Mary prayed also, though more briefly, for she was not used to audible prayer as I was. She asked that God would bless our home and make us a blessing to each other. She asked for particular blessings on me, her husband. It was not an easy thing for either of us at first, but from the beginning it was a blessed thing for us both. We found that when husband and wife pray that way together, they cannot get very far apart."

Prayer in parenthood is a vital force. There is nothing more challenging, uplifting and frightening than that moment when the young mother and father, holding in their arms that pink, crying, eternal bundle of humanity, cry out "This is our child! God help us to be worthy to guide and shape this life in the years to come." At the request of my publisher, I am including here a "Prayer for a New Baby" as recorded on Word Records' "When Home Is Heaven", (W–3118):*

PRAYER FOR A NEW BABY

O God, Great Father, we bless Thee for this frightening, this thrilling, this tremendous gift of a child.

This child is the dearest gift we could offer Thee, outside of ourselves, since this is flesh of our flesh, blood of our blood, bone of our bone, and soul of our soul. It is ours to guide, this small eternal thing. Its destiny lies in our hands. In a sense we shape its tomorrow. It knows not whence it came or whither it is going. The reason for living is ours—to teach and to explain—be sure we ourselves know what it is.

Now we place this child in Thine arms. It is Thine. We but assist Thee in its tutelage. It is merely given to us for training and for nurture. As now we dedicate it to Thee, we launch this tiny

*"A Prayer for a New Baby" copyright © 1968 by Louis H. Evans, Sr.

ship, with its little three-inch sail, upon a great and stormy sea of life.

May Thy Word be its compass; the wind of Thy goodwill fill its sail; Christ's hand be upon the tiny rudder and through storm and flood bring it to its desired haven in Thine own good day. Strengthen this little body, making it strong to bear the pressures and vicissitudes of life. Make keen its mind on the emery wheels of learning and the precepts of this home. May we nurture it in the things of God and the Spirit that its little soul may keep pace with its body and its mind. May it grow as Christ grew "in wisdom and stature and favor with God and man."

When older, this child shall need a critic, but for a few years now it shall need an example. May little be seen in our lives to offend or to counteract the high ideal to which we gave birth that day. May the tears that will flow from those eyes we love but serve to wash and to cleanse its vision. May struggles but tend to strengthen the fibers of the soul, and may all of life's pressures bid it press more closely to God—Who is our strength. May this child thus be the fruition of our highest hopes, our bravest dreams and the answer to our extravagant prayer.

Some day, when maturity beckons, teach us how to take the young hand from our own and place it in Thy hand, Oh God, for then it is Thine alone to guide, to lead and to sustain. Bless the day when the cage is opened and the bird flies free and may its flight be immediately high in the heavens and on the pinions of God, and may it make its nest in the highlands of the Lord forever. This we ask of Thee, Great Fatherly Heart of whose love ours is but a humble reflection and whose children we are. Amen.

Parental prayers with the family. How soon should we pray *with* a child? It might be surprising to know how early a young heart and soul might be affected by our intercessions. Dorothy Wilson, in her book on child psychology and religious education, quotes the following story: "The child of an atheistic father and a religious mother used to listen to his mother singing in a low voice to him as he lay in his cradle. As he grew a little older he noticed that she was singing of or to some Invisible Friend, but he could understand no more than that. Yet when frightened of any vague terror, he remembered his mother's tone and attitude at these times and felt peaceful and secure in the protection of this Mysterious Being. When he was only three years old they moved to a new house. His mother, whose faith was overcome by misfortune, came under the atheistic sway of her husband and spoke no more of God to the child. He was only eight years old when his mother fell seriously ill, but he turned at once for help to this Invisible Friend, and was assured of the recovery of his mother (which did take place) and always, after that, believed in and prayed to God."

Here, before three years of age, we find a lasting religious impression made almost entirely by example. Since reading this story I have done a very simple thing which I recommend to you. Instead of praying silently for your children, and in another room, pray aloud by their cot. I believe it is valuable, even if a little child is asleep, to pray aloud at his bed.

Teaching the child to pray is one of the important challenges and privileges parents face. Prayer ought to become as normal as breathing—as normal as talking to a parent.

But there are some *barriers to audible prayer.* One is timidity and self-consciousness. We have an idea that prayer should be some sort of spiritual oration, or impressive, poetic dialogue, whereas it is merely "the sincere desire of the soul expressed." Too many prayers are made to impress people rather than to have simple speech with God. It ought, with reverence, to become as natural as a talk with parent or worthy friend, since the recommended approach is to say, "Our Father. . . ."

One of the blocks to audible prayer is the often prevalent idea that to be reverent we should use King James English. Many find it unnatural to use the "wouldsts, thous, and mightests" of the King James English and wish to avoid embarrassment. Why should the language of the seventeenth century be more pleasing to God than the tongue of the twentieth? When I pro-

posed to my girl I did not do it in Chaucer's or
King James' English—it would have been unnatural, artificial, affected. The reverence lies
not in the syllables nor the style, but in the spirit
of the prayer.

Let us not put too much pressure on the child
to pray. When our children are asked the question, "Would you like to pray—say grace?" they
might answer with an embarrassed, "No."
Later on they may say: "I think I would like to
pray this time."

Someday it should come naturally to them if
the catechism's definition of prayer is true:
"Prayer is an offering up of our desires unto
God, for things agreeable to his will, in the name
of Christ, with confession of our sins, and thank-
ful acknowledgment of his mercies." Then let us
keep prayer honest and simple for our children's sake and God's.

Many teach their children to pray by using a
book of prayers for children which they read out
loud. This helps them to overcome the fear of
the sound of their own voices and their inability
to phrase the desires of their hearts—something
that doesn't come easily at first. Of course, I
think that our children's natural prayers are the
best—prayers like, "Dear God, bless my
mommy and daddy and all the family and the
whole world. And please, God, take good care of
yourself because if anything happens to you,

we'll all be in the soup." What a testimony to the importance of God's sovereignty! I recall my little daughter's prayer one Sunday, "Dear Jesus, bless my daddy and may he have a good preach." How that helped! My son, Lou, prayed at his mother's knee, "Dear Jesus, bless my daddy when he preaches and may his sermon perspire the people." He must have felt his mother jerk a little for he said, "Mother, I guess that wasn't the right word, was it?" She replied, "We will leave it that way, son. I guess you meant "inspire," but your father would be happy if, after the sermon, his parishioners would get to work a little more and perspire a little more."

Let us help them, in their prayers, to *avoid selfishness*. I will admit that the first person pronoun used in, "Now *I* lay *me* down to sleep, *I* pray the Lord *my* soul to keep . . ." can seem a little selfish. The letter *I* is the narrowest word in the dictionary and should be used sparingly. When you pray say, *"Our* Father." From the Lord's Prayer we see that the pronouns which refer to the speaker are plural in their expression of desires. For example, "Give us this day. . . ."When we learn to use plural pronouns in our prayers, there might also be a metamorphosis—a change—in our petitions themselves.

What has happened to *family prayer?* Someone said that the family altar is as hard to find today as a four-leaf clover in a pasture. One father pled "over-busyness" to me. But prayer is absolutely essential for building a healthy family life. The souls of the family live on the "living bread" and on the "sincere milk of his word," our deeper thirst is quenched only by the "living water." As parents, we are appalled at the undernourishment of young bodies. Some families will spend at least one and a half hours a day with their three meals, but they cannot find ten minutes once a day for the "living bread." A Sunday School lesson for the children or one Sunday sermon a week is considered sufficient by some families. Imagine the human body trying to survive, much less be healthy and vigorous, on one meal a week! No wonder the souls today are restless, starved, and too weak to stand up to temptation; no wonder they faint before the pressures of modern life.

In many homes there is a *mirror* of some sort in almost every room. It allows us to see ourselves as we really are—but the effects vary. The Bible is like that. Dwight L. Moody once said, "This book will keep you from sin, and sin will keep you from this book." Before it we stand as we are—just as God sees us—not like a retouched photograph, but with each imperfection showing. The Bible applauds our virtues, points out our vices and woos us to great beauty

of character and a classic Christlikeness. Without it we can become spiritually unkempt and
fail to see ourselves as God sees us.

A girl had hastily finished her breakfast,
readied herself to be off to school. Her hair was
untidy, her dress awry. Her mother complained, "Darling, you look like a witch. What's
the matter?" She replied, "My mirror broke the
other day, and I wasn't aware of how I looked
today." Suppose she had made a reference to
the Bible that mirrored her as God and others
saw her day by day? Without a daily reading of
God's Word and prayer, we men might go out to
meet the world *spiritually* unshaven, the linen of
our lives soiled, the hair of our thoughts
tousled—quite unfit to meet the world as
groomed sons of God.

Many Christian women look well-dressed and
nicely groomed. They ought to: "Women, adorn
yourselves" is God's command and in that outward sense they are a credit to the Christian
family. But how many Christian women spend
hours on their physical appearance and don't
take time to rub the cream of kindness into their
character, powder out the lines of care with the
brush of devotion, smooth the tangles in the
hair of their disposition so that when they meet
the world they not only *look* right, but *feel*
right?

Some people would not think of going out to

live the day without consulting their horoscope
or astrological chart, yet they give not five minutes to consult the Word of God; it's as though
those dusty, rocky planets had more to do with
planning their lives than the God who placed
them in their orbits, as though the signs of
Pisces and Aquarius had more to say about their
behavior than the Son of God. No wonder the
lines of worry and the strain of uncertainty fur-
row our faces and crease our countenances.

To avoid spiritual undernourishment, we
need to spend more time with God in prayer.
William D. Longstaff gives us some good advice
in the well-known hymn, "Take Time to Be
Holy":

Take time to be holy; the world rushes on;
Spend much time in secret with Jesus alone.
By looking to Jesus, like Him thou shalt be;
Thy friends in thy conduct *His likeness* shall see.

Quarreling, enmity, and crude thoughtless-
ness destroy the power of prayer. Peter, in his
first epistle, admonishes husbands with these
words, "Likewise ye husbands, dwell with [your
wives] according to knowledge [understanding
them—trying to] giving honour unto the
wife . . . and as being heirs together of the grace
of life; that your prayers be not hindered" (3:7,
KJV). The absence of this thoughtful together-
ness cramps the power of prayer. In Matthew

we learn that Jesus says, "If two [or three] of you agree ... about anything they ask, it will be done for them by my Father in heaven" (18:19, RSV). God, then, is more likely to hear the request of two together than each alone in his or her divisive, selfish requesting. The closeness of our relationships with each other has a lot to do with our nearness to God.

We live in a day of tremendous pressure, and many homes lie broken as the result of it. But there is a wonderful kind of healing for this brokenness that comes when the family worships and prays together—a healing for the pressures and strain of city life, the din of the factory, the frustrations of the business office, the rush of school life, the problems of dealing with people and the frantic speed of the directionless life. In family prayer, there is help for the self-pitying older person, the spoiled child, the nervous mother, and the troubled adolescent. The problems of our psychotic, neurotic age—the uncertainty of world and local affairs—double the need of the adhesive of family worship and prayer.

Here is the story of a family who experienced the healing effects of family worship:

He came into his pastor's office beaten and discouraged. He said, "Pastor, there is something the matter with our family—it's going to pieces. I'm desperate. Our high-school daughter is a thankless brat. She never says, 'Thank you.' She thinks I am an 'oddball' and her mother is a 'square.' My wife—she is a fussbudget, intensely tired, and never quiet. She has more buttons, badges, scoreboards, memberships, and programs than you can shake a stick at. She comes home every night nervous, tight, and terrible. Myself—I am one of those 'misunderstood businessmen,' sorry for myself when I come home at night. Gruff as a bear, I ensconce myself behind a newspaper, and when the television is turned on, I shout, 'Turn that thing off. I deserve some quiet!' I am touchy as a sore boil. Our dear little home is falling apart—and I don't want that. What can we do?"

The pastor smiled understandingly, reached back and took from his shelf one of the copies of small family devotions he kept there and said, "Take this and use it. It's simple. Any one of you can read it in turn—the scripture, the explanation, and then the printed prayer if you are not ready with your own. Take turns. Start right now—you might not have much more time!"

He did. One evening the father was reading from Psalm 103, a masterpiece on gratitude. During the prayer the high-school daughter bit her lip and prayed, "God, forgive me, thoughtless brat that I am!" When her turn came one evening, she read 1 Corinthians 13, that masterpiece on love, and the prayer that followed it. While she read, the husband slipped his hand under the table and found his wife's waiting hand, and for the first time in two years, husband and wife held hands.

It had *happened*—the strain abated; the family stress was eased, their nerves were soothed, and peace was restored. Two weeks later the man came into the pastor's office and said, "It worked, sir, it worked! What was the matter with us?" The pastor smiled and, student of the soul as he was, said, "You all were just *God-hungry*. You had starved yourselves spiritually. Never try that again!"

The fruits of the well-groomed and well-kept spirit are love, joy, peace, longsuffering, gentleness, meekness, self-control. The weeds of the unkempt, uncultivated, neglected human heart are uninspired, uninstructed, uninviting, untended, unled, unlovable, unmanageable, unmannered, unmindful, unmelodious, unmirthful, unobliging, uncheerful, and unchecked.

When prayer is a regular part of our lives, we keep the weeds controlled and the fruit of the spirit can flourish.

What a keen student of the human spirit Richard C. Trench was as he penned these lines:

PRAYER

Lord, what a change within us one short hour
Spent in Thy presence will avail to make!
What heavy burdens from our bosoms take!
What parched grounds refresh as with a shower!

We kneel, and all around us seems to lower;
We rise, and all, the distant and the near,
Stands forth in sunny outline, brave and clear;
We kneel, how weak! We rise, how full of power!
Why, therefore, should we do ourselves this wrong,
Or others—that we are not always strong—
That we are sometimes overborne with care—
That we should ever weak or heartless be,
Anxious or troubled—when with us is prayer,
And joy and strength and courage are with Thee?

Let us make this our prayer: *"Lord of love, bless our home. Make me easy to live with: quick to praise and slow to blame. Teach us that with money we may build a house; adding love to that house, it becomes a home; adding Christ to that home, it becomes a castle royal; adding God, it becomes a Temple. Remind us that, made in Thine image as we are, we cannot live at our happiest and at our highest until our homes become Thy temples. O come to us, abide with us, our Lord Immanuel. In the name of Christ, great lover of our souls, Amen."*